WESCAPE TO THE
Wine Country

California's Napa, Sonoma, and Mendocino

Photography by Robert Holmes

Text by Thom Elkjer

Fodor's

FODOR'S TRAVEL PUBLICATIONS
NEW YORK • TORONTO • LONDON • SYDNEY • AUCKLAND • WWW.FODORS.COM

Escape to the Wine Country
COPYRIGHT © 2002 BY FODORS LLC
Photographs copyright © 2002 by Robert Holmes
Fodor's is a registered trademark of Random House, Inc.

While every care has been taken to ensure the accuracy of the
information in this guide, time brings change, and consequently
the publisher cannot accept responsibility for errors that may
occur. Call ahead to verify prices and other information.

First Edition
ISBN 0-679-00918-3
ISSN 1537-5579

Special Sales
Fodor's Travel Publications are available at special discounts
for bulk purchases for sales promotions or premiums. Special
editions, including personalized covers, excerpts of existing
guides, and corporate imprints, can be created in large
quantities for special needs. For more information, contact your
local bookseller or write to Special Markets, Fodor's Travel
Publications, 280 Park Ave., New York, NY 10017. Inquiries from
Canada should be directed to your local Canadian bookseller or
sent to Random House of Canada, Ltd., Marketing Dept., 2775
Matheson Boulevard East, Mississauga, Ontario L4W 4P7.
Inquiries from the United Kingdom should be sent to Fodor's
Travel Publications, 20 Vauxhall Bridge Road, London, England
SW1V 2SA.

PRINTED IN GERMANY
10 9 8 7 6 5 4 3 2 1

Library of Congress Cataloging-in-Publication Data available
upon request.

Acknowledgments
From Robert Holmes: A special thanks to my daughters,
Emma and Hannah, and my wife, Bobbie, for accompanying me
on many forays into the wine country, and for their tolerance
of my absences when they were unable to go with me, particularly
as they knew what they were missing. To my mother, Marjorie
Holmes, and to the memory of my father, Maurice Holmes,
who encouraged me to explore the world at an early age. A big
thank you to Tigist Getachew for her skillfull art direction that
always makes me look good. And, not least, a huge thanks to
Fabrizio La Rocca, whose passion and exceptional support made
this book a reality.

From Thom Elkjer: A deep bow of inspired respect to
Fabrizio La Rocca for creating this series, and to Bob Holmes
for so generously sharing his total mastery of travel
photography – may all books be this much fun and look this
good. Heartfelt thanks to everyone in the wine country who
stopped to talk, agreed to pose, opened early, stayed late, or
found us a bed/seat/table/ticket at the last minute. Endless,
loving gratitude to Antoinette for sharing the creative path and,
often, lighting the way.

Credits
Creative Director and Series Editor: Fabrizio La Rocca
Editorial Director: Karen Cure
Art Director: Tigist Getachew

Editor: Diane Mehta
Editorial Assistant: Dennis Sarlo
Production/Manufacturing: C. R. Bloodgood, Robert B. Shields
Maps: David Lindroth, Inc.

Other Escape Guides
Escape to the Amalfi Coast • Escape to the American Desert
Escape to the Hawaiian Islands • Escape to Ireland
Escape to Morocco • Escape to Provence
Escape to the Riviera • Escape to Tuscany
Available in bookstores

Most books on the travel shelves are either long on the nitty-gritty and short on evocative photographs, or the other way around. We at Fodor's think that the different balance in this slim volume is just perfect, rather like the intersection of the most luscious magazine article and a sensible, down-to-earth guidebook. On the road, the useful pages at the end of the book are practically all you need. For the planning, roam through the stories and the photographs up front: each one reveals a key facet of the vast and variegated northern California wine country on the western edge of the United States, and conveys a sense of place that will take you there before you go. Each page opens up to exceptional experiences; each spread leads you to the spirit of the wine country at its purest.

Some of these places are sure to beckon. You may yearn to cruise the coast on a crab boat, or long to ride a horse into the countryside that adventurer Jack London once loved. You may consider bidding on a rare wine at the Winesong! wine auction, or exploring the grand Niebaum-Coppola Estate Winery, owned by Francis Ford Coppola. You can settle into a mud or mineral bath in Calistoga or visit world-class art collections. Discover the spirit of Sonoma, with its historic adobe buildings. Feast your eyes on the golden mustard that blooms every winter in Napa. Then end the day sipping sparkling wine on a terrace as dusk sets the landscape abaze in pink and purple.

To capture the essence of the wine country, author Thom Elkjer and photographer Robert Holmes visited scores of wineries and saw many charming vineyards across northern California. They also took a balloon ride, had massages and mud baths, rode horses among fragrant oaks, and ate a lot of fresh, local specialties. One thing they're sure of: even after years of covering the wine country, on any given trip they find the countryside filled with a rustic, pastoral drama that shifts with each season, and new places worth exploring. But what keeps them returning, they insist, are the hospitable and sophisticated people they meet during their travels.

Follow in the footsteps of Holmes and Elkjer, and you too will get a sense of the variety and magic of the northern California landscape. Forget your projects and deadlines, and escape to the Wine Country. You owe it to yourself.

—The Editors

AS DAWN SLIPS OVER THE EASTERN MOUNTAINS INTO NAPA VALLEY, A GIANT creature picks itself up, shakes itself awake, and slowly rises from the cold ground. Taut, vibrating with energy, and towering over you, this patchwork-quilt mantle of colors engenders fascination, not fear—it's a hot-air balloon about to take you aloft. Passengers clamber into the wicker basket as pilot Jim Marshall pulls a lever and a hot jet of propane-blue flame roars up into the space above you. Once everyone's aboard, he fires the jets again and the balloon seems to lift itself, as if by magic. A thousand feet up the view is striking—and different—in every direction. The warming sun crests the steep cliffs that punctuate the Vacas Mountain to the east. At the north end of the valley the towns of St. Helena and Calistoga are still slumbering in deep shadow; Mount St. Helena hulks above them. To the west, long fingers of sea-sent fog

Dawn Flight

BALLOONING OVER NAPA VALLEY

A balloon's slow, stately passage reveals the wine country's seamless blend of nature with civilization, the sheer variety of hills and villages, and the sensual shades of sunrise.

hold Sonoma County firmly in their grip. Below you, in picturesque procession, pass vineyards, trees, wineries, small towns, country lanes, and the occasional hilltop mansion. Although you're moving, everything seems still because your speed is the same as the wind's. Content, everyone has fallen silent. Ultimately, as you watch your shadow grow larger against the side of a hill, you realize you're descending—into a clearing surrounded by some of the most precious vineyard acres in the world. Marshall gives the jets one more blast and the balloon touches down softly, with hardly a bump. Everything is so solid around you—for a moment it seems impossible that you were really flying.

As dawn breaks in the wine country,
a ground crew fires the powerful jets of
pulsating, multicolored balloons ready
to commence their open-air flight over
the Napa Valley.

NATIVE AMERICANS CALLED IT *TA LA HA LU SI*, OR "OVEN PLACE." GEYSERS COURSING up through layers of volcanic ash created natural mudbaths. Today the area is called Calistoga—it's the northernmost town in Napa Valley, and it's home to hot-spring spas that offer a modern version of "Oven Place." At Indian Springs Resort the steaming heat and black ash come from just outside the walls of the historic spa building erected by Calistoga's founder, gold-rush millionaire Sam Brannan. Inside the warm, sulphur-scented spa, you begin an hour-long treatment in a large bathtub, where you are buried to the neck in hot mud. It's hard to believe this heavy black mass was powder-light volcanic ash before it mixed with steaming geyser water. The combination draws impurities out of your pores and tension out of your muscles, easing you into a gentle siesta. Fifteen minutes seem to pass in seconds, and then it's

Steam Heat

INDIAN SPRINGS RESORT, CALISTOGA

Twenty-five years ago, Calistoga spas were chock full of European immigrants. Now health-conscious visitors of all ages have taken to the muds and minerals.

time for a cleansing soak in a thermal pool. In contrast to the mud, the water feels weightless. The minerals that make it feel so soft smell pungent, almost medicinal. In the next stage, a quiet quarter-hour passes in a steam room, where the soft hissing of pressurized vapor is another invitation to sink into pure relaxation. The cool water in the tall glass beside you, with its bright, fresh lemon, energizes you. After a shower there's time to cool down, wrapped tightly in a light blanket, before stepping outside to stroll under tall, swaying palm trees to the Olympic-sized pool. No one swims any laps, though—the water, supplied by geysers, stays at a languorous 102 degrees. Giant inner tubes bob on the surface, big enough to for you to stretch out on and let the heat continue to cast its invigorating spell.

Mudbath treatments stimulate circulation in one of your body's most important organs: the skin. Deep relaxation is a natural side effect, making the post-mudbath period perfect for a massage or a nap.

A GARDENER KNEELS BENEATH A SNOW ANGEL ROSEBUSH, WHICH lifts its white flowers to the warmth of the sun that drenches Ferrari-Carano Vineyards and Winery. Overhead, an octagonal pavilion provides shade from the afternoon heat. To the left, a waterfall splashes into a rock pool where bright-red carp dart in and out of rippling shadows. To the right, a burbling brook flows past the roses toward a bed of multicolored begonias. Everything is calm, almost transcendently still, as the gardener examines each leaf and cane of the rose until he is satisfied and moves on. You move on, too, past a dwarf balsam fir tree, a Japanese weeping cherry, a saucer magnolia and crepe myrtle, the contorted mulberry, and scores of other trees, shrubs, and perennials, including some of California's only thriving Portuguese cork oaks.

Estate of Serenity

SONOMA'S SPECTACULAR WINE ESTATE GARDEN

As many as 18,000 tulips and irises bloom in early spring here; the undulating colors transform the gardens.

Everywhere footpaths, footbridges, and colored borders link gardens. It's hard to believe such lushness exists at the head of dusty Dry Creek Valley—or that a mid-sized winery maintains a staff of six full-time gardeners to keep it all so immaculate. Gardening is a passion of Rhonda Carano, who founded and designed Ferrari-Carano with her husband Don. Everything about the property, including the 25,000-square-foot Villa Fiore ("Flower House"), seems a reflection of the gardens, where a formal structure tames natural beauty. Climbing up a gentle slope, you come to a balustraded terrace that yields vistas of vines and thousands of annuals ablaze in a French parterre. Through the mullioned windows of the tasting room you see bottles arrayed on a marble-topped bar. One bears the name "Tresor." It's Ferrari-Carano's flagship wine, with a label depicting a fiery sunset. The name means "treasure"—which suits its ripe, cassis-like flavors of black cherries, cedar forest, and dark Dutch chocolate.

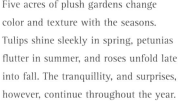

Five acres of plush gardens change color and texture with the seasons. Tulips shine sleekly in spring, petunias flutter in summer, and roses unfold late into fall. The tranquillity, and surprises, however, continue throughout the year.

LACY CURTAINS OF GRAY MIST HANG IN TOWERING REDWOOD TREES AS you cruise a two-lane road through river-cut hills on a morning in early March. You have left the crowded freeways and ventured into the deep-green countryside of the Russian River Valley, one of America's most celebrated wine regions, renowned for its dense, dark-berry Pinot Noirs and complex, honey-colored Chardonnays. One weekend a year, the region's vintners offer visitors a chance to taste directly from the oak barrels, where freshly fermented young wines mature into smooth, complex elixirs ready for bottling. Often winemakers are still deciding how to blend the contents of their barrels into finished wines, so you can taste their work in progress and discuss the possibilities. You can also get an early read on the recent vintage by tasting wines

Back Roads & Barrel Samples

BARREL TASTING ON THE RUSSIAN RIVER WINE ROAD, SONOMA

In wintertime, after grapes have been picked and when the vines go dormant, winemakers coax their new-born wines through fermentation and ponder how to age and blend them.

that have been in the barrel only a few months. Here, around the towns of Guerneville, Forestville, and Sebastopol, there are no faux châteaus, no tour buses. At one of the region's landmark wineries, Davis Bynum, you enter down a gravel drive past a small farmhouse and park beneath a spreading oak. The winery occupies an old redwood barn weathered silver and bronze. Through the doorway you can see the barrels lying on their sides. The winemaker dips a thin siphon called a "thief" into the bunghole at the top of the barrel, then releases a small amount of unblended, estate-grown Pinot Noir into a glass. The freshness of its bright, clear strawberry flavors is like a sweet flash of summer in the dead of winter, a reminder that, like wine itself, the wine country is always a work in progress, one worth visiting in every season.

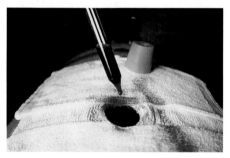

Oak barrels look rough and rugged, yet they're hand-made from oak from special forests in America and France and "toasted" inside to impart subtly different qualities to aging wine.

Winesong!

A MEETING OF MUSIC, FOOD, AND WINE IN MENDOCINO

THROUGH THE FOREST COMES THE TIMELESS SOUND OF WOOD PIPES PLAYING A REPEATED, HYPNOTIC tune. The path toward the music gently rises and falls through a green maze of soaring redwood trees, beds of giant rhododendrons, and rare plants. For a moment it's like a scene from *A Midsummer Night's Dream*. Then you round a bend and see master piper Sean Folsom playing a Tunisian bagpipe called a *mízwíd*. Behind him, along paths leading in every direction, servers at colorfully decorated tables dispense tasting portions of Mendocino wine and local foods. The plush, dark fruit flavors of a Pacific Star Zinfandel marry perfectly with the tangy spices in a grilled organic sausage. The forest is part of the Mendocino Coast Botanical Gardens, and the purveyors are all here for Winesong!, Mendocino County's annual charity wine auction. Time whizzes by as you sample recent vintages from boutique wineries as well as brand-name labels while listening to intimate jazz, classical, and folk

At the pre-auction tasting among the Edenic colors of the botanical gardens, wineries showcase current releases—major varietals and proprietary blends, everything your taste buds can adore or admire.

music under a green canopy of trees. When the auction gets under way, everyone heads for a vast open-air tent where festive tables are set with bottles of wine, gourmet cheeses, artisanal bread, and chocolate-dipped strawberries. Celebrated vintners Ann Colgin and Dick Grace, famed chef and author Narsai David, and comedian David Reynolds are among the celebrities in attendance. The rapid-fire calls of the auctioneers rise above the conversation around you. Soon you get into the spirit, raising your paddle to bid on a magnum of Screaming Eagle Cabernet Sauvignon and joining in the crowd's roar of approval when it raises thousands of dollars in seconds.

AT A TIME WHEN MANY OTHERS ARE LONGING FOR SPRING AND ENDURING THE final weeks of winter, Napa Valley residents celebrate the wine country's secret season—the glorious few weeks when ubiquitous mustard blooms in the vinerows, creating a lush yellow carpet across the valley floor. The time has come for the Napa Valley Mustard Festival, a weeks-long multi-venue event in which arts and crafts, music, photography, food-and-wine pairings, and a mustard-themed market fair come together—with plenty of wine-drenched dinners and lavish parties. Champion mustard makers arrive to pit their mustards against those of their rivals, and chefs showcase their latest mustard-themed inventions. Mustard, a cover crop planted between vineyard rows to hold and replenish the soil during winter rains, flips the valley's summer color scheme on its head: grasses that were dry gold in August are verdant,

Napa's Secret Season

NAPA VALLEY MUSTARD FESTIVAL

Wild, passionate yellows color the wintering vine rows as spring edges closer and the entire valley shimmers.

while once-green vineyards have turned golden. The mustard grows so high you can wade through it, though the wet ground makes that a temptation better avoided. To see it, take to the richly scenic back road that locals consider their private highway, the Silverado Trail. This slightly elevated two-lane road gives you the full range of views of the mustard: close-ups of vineyards along the highway, medium shots up and down adjacent hillsides, and long views out across the valley floor. If you find yourself constantly pulling out your camera, you'll be in good company. All over the valley, professional and amateur photographers alike are shooting pictures to enter in the upcoming Photo Finish, a photo contest and dinner-dance that winds up the Mustard Festival. On that final, exhilarating evening, photographers reveal the many passionate colors and varieties of the region's geography, the wine flows seemingly without end, and the music and dancing continue late into the night.

Winter undresses the twisted, gnarled arms
of countless grapevines and reveals their ages.
The thicker the vine, the longer it has been
producing wine. Vines will live 100 years, or
more, but most are replaced at half that age.

Whimsical Jimtown

ODDBALL ARTIFACTS IN THE ALEXANDER VALLEY, SONOMA

AT THE JIMTOWN STORE, THE MERCHANDISE RISES FROM THE WOOD-PLANK FLOOR TO THE CEILING hung with seasonal decorations, mismatched stools line the tin counter in the front window, and time-worn signs on the walls urge you to "Get in Here and Eat." There's almost too much to take in: a red formica–topped table near the deli counter, balsa-wood gliders and paper-doll kits, and odd candies on the counter by the cash register. From the dogs waiting patiently outside the front door to the cream soda in the cold case, Jimtown evokes memories of the country store America grew up with. Being here is like being a kid again, except that at Jimtown premium wine and cold-pressed olive oil keep company with the wax lips and Slinky toys, and sandwiches come with spicy house-made Asian peanut spread instead of bland mayonnaise. Outside, the sky continually changes color above the vineyards and willow trees that line the Russian River. This is a place where all the characters of wine-

country life make an appearance: baseball-capped winegrowers in pick-up trucks, tourists in a 1949 white Packard limousine, mothers and children stopping in for an after-school snack. Some disappear through a doorway in the back, past a rack of brightly colored Mexican oilcloths, into a back room full of rustic antiques, a cozy patio beneath a grape arbor, and a tiny garden house filled with still more antiques and artifacts. The wineries you planned to visit are just up the road. But it's hard to leave this quirky slice of the past. After some shopping, you can settle near the front window with a glass of Murphy-Goode Chardonnay, among the oldfangled merchandise, in a nostalgic reverie.

Sample delectable, homemade snacks, and browse among the charming clutter for toys, antiques, and virtually anything you can't find elsewhere.

"I MADE A SMALL FORTUNE IN THE WINE BUSINESS," BEGINS THE diminutive man at the podium, "and I'll tell you how I did it: I started with a large fortune." Laughter echoes through the underground caves of Clos Pegase Winery. For the next hour, the winery's owner, Jan Shrem, narrates his multimedia presentation "A Bacchanalian History of Wine Seen Through 4,000 Years of Art," which features images of paintings, sculptures, and winemaking tools from 40 centuries and 10 countries. Many real-life originals hang in the winery buildings and are scattered around the grounds, including modern masterpieces by Henry Moore and Richard Serra. They are fitting ornaments for a winery the *Washington Post* once called "America's first temple of wine as art." Another winery owner with a world-class art collection is Donald Hess—

The Eyes Have It

ART AMONG THE VINES IN THE NAPA VALLEY

Mildred Howard gives wine bottles a whole new meaning in her *Memory Garden, Phase 1*, a mixed-media installation that incorporates 4,000 bottles of all colors and sizes.

he combines them in his Hess Collection, 10 miles south of Clos Pegase. High above the tasting room of the century-old stone winery, deep dormer windows illuminate austere, formal galleries filled with works by Frank Stella, Robert Motherwell, and Francis Bacon. Only Leopoldo Maler's burning typewriter, titled *Hommage*, hints that the passionate, exacting Hess—who personally supervises the hanging of the galleries—has a sense of humor. The feeling could not be more different 15 miles away, in the di Rosa Preserve, where former journalist Rene di Rosa created a haven for birds and wildlife and then populated it with a different kind of creature: contemporary works by California artists. Many are designed to amuse or confront us, much as di Rosa did when he was a notorious San Francisco journalist. Today he's making us think with images, not words: a steel cow grazing on a lake, a 1967 Pontiac with the head of a horse, and intricate religious images applied in oil paint and gold leaf to a skateboard.

Wild twisted sculptures, gigantic jokes,
carefully executed paintings, bizarre
and obscure shapes—the only thing you
won't find is a lack of imagination.

WRANGLER JULIE VADER TWISTS AROUND AND STUDIES THE LINE OF horses and riders behind her. Satisfied, she softly spurs her horse and heads out into open chaparral. Mounted on a mahogany mare on a sultry summer day, you glide behind her—your guide—through a fragrant grove of eucalyptus trees planted by Jack London, one of America's best-known authors and adventurers at the turn of the 20th century. Back then his novels—such as *Call of the Wild*, about survival in the Arctic—brought America's rugged western frontier into living rooms across the country. The process reverses in Jack London State Historical Park, where many visitors come to leave civilization behind and ride out into London's world the way he did: tall in the saddle. As you emerge into open country, a trail skirts a sloping Merlot vineyard and

Western Frontier

RIDING JACK LONDON'S RANCH IN SONOMA

Trails in the 800-acre park wind through emerald vinelands and across ruggedly forested hills. Your reward: a sensuous, stunning panaroma of the Valley of the Moon.

heads up into the hills above Sonoma's Valley of the Moon. Such vistas inspired London to acquire hundreds of acres and build a home. "The grapes on a score of rolling hills are red with autumn flame," he wrote in *John Barleycorn*. "Across Sonoma Mountain wisps of sea fog are stealing. The afternoon sun smoulders in the drowsy sky. I have everything to make me glad I am alive." Like London, you're glad to be on a horse—so you can drink in the view without watching where you step, as you move down the rocky trail through classic California woodland. Oaks, redwoods, and buckeyes give off earthy aromas and provide sun-dappled shade. In the vineyards up ahead two wild turkeys strut below bunches of low-hanging Cabernet Sauvignon. Jack London might have unholstered a rifle and bagged the birds for dinner. Instead, you break out your camera and shoot them silently, capturing your own piece of the western splendor that London himself named Beauty Ranch.

A ROOSTER'S CROWING OUTSIDE THE WINDOW AND THE FIRST RAYS OF DAWN rouse you in your snug cottage in a fragrant, riverside orchard. It's morning at the Apple Farm in Mendocino's Anderson Valley, and you don't want to miss a moment. On the golden, oak-studded hillsides above, the vineyards are awakening, too. Outside, ripe apples drop into wicker baskets as pickers maneuver tall, three-legged ladders high into the crown of an heirloom Pink Pearl apple tree. You bite into a freshly picked apple and marvel at the soft, dusty rose color inside. Sally Schmitt appears in the kitchen doorway and waves to let you know the coffee is hot, the fresh bread cut for toasting, and the homemade jam ready for spreading. Nearby, a group of colorfully plumed Americauna chickens struts past overflowing herb beds and into a rose garden where fresh blossoms glow in the sun. The way to the kitchen leads through fruitless mulberry

Orchard Idyll

THE APPLE FARM, ANDERSON VALLEY, MENDOCINO

The Apple Farm grows about 60 varieties of this tangy, red-sexy fruit. Try the 1924 hybrid Kidds Orange Red and the Yellow Winter Banana— so mild it almost tastes like a pear.

trees woven into an arch-shaped, multichambered arbor of green leaves and blue sky. In the light-filled kitchen, Sally and her daughter Karen are preparing for one of their Thursday cooking classes; you make a mental note to sign up before your next visit. As they work, they suggest ways to enjoy the day: a walk among old-growth redwoods in Hendy Woods State Park across the Navarro River, a dip in the sun-splashed swimming hole under the bridge. They also toss out tips on which apple varieties are best for baking, juicing, and storing; you take your new knowledge out to the orchard. Strolling between the trees and the meandering river, you now notice how the different kinds of apples ripen at their own pace. The Golden Delicious hanging above you are growing into their signature harvest color, but the Sierra Beauties, still more green than red, are weeks away from autumnal perfection.

From breezy late summer through fiery autumn, the Apple Farm harvests a slew of luscious, organic, heirloom apples. You can taste them as they ripen and are brought to the farm's open-air market, where lip-licking cider, juice, jams, and sweet-and-spicy chutneys will tempt you.

THE ENTRANCE TO VILLA CA'TOGA LOOKS LIKE A DUSTY LANE OFF a back street. It's the first trick played on you by master artist Carlo Marchiori, a modern-day Prospero working his magic in the wine country. At the driveway's last turn, California becomes Italy. Through a vine-covered pergola appears the facade of a grand Palladian villa with a central balcony and flanking loggias. Draw closer—giant masks out of *commedia dell'arte* leer from fluted pedestals. A Venetian lion, carved in stone, seems to smile and snarl simultaneously. Inside, two-story sculptures hold up the ceiling, despite dangerous-looking cracks in their stone. A costumed 17th-century courtier comes toward you through a curtained door, accompanied by his dog, a young Bazenji. It's all a fantastic illusion, a painted tour de force that Marchiori calls "trompe l'oeil for the

Master of Illusion

CARLO MARCHIORI'S VILLA IN CALISTOGA, NAPA VALLEY

"Ca'Toga"—not only is it an abbreviation of the town's name; in Marchiori's native Venetian argot it is a sly, complex pun combining "my little country place," "house of exotic attractions," and "home of my dog Togo."

soul, not just the eye." He offers a witty commentary as he walks his weekly Saturday tour group upstairs and pushes open the door of a small bedroom, painted from the point of view of a caged bird. Outside the cage looms a huge, hungry cat, peering intently in at the bird—you. In another bedroom the ceiling illustrates the story of Icarus, the mythical character who flew too near the sun on wings of feathers and wax. Lie down on the bed—from that vantage point Icarus plunges down straight at you. In room after room, Marchiori's dark sense of humor comes across in lush, intoxicating murals—such as cows that melt into surrealistic poems. The illusions continue outdoors: a tiled swimming pool re-creates the ancient baths of imperial Rome, and a row of Doric columns standing among broken pediments and fallen cornices reminds us of the Latin poet Horace's dictum *Vita brevis, ars longa*—life is short, art endures.

Pick a century: Renaissance-style art and architecture, Classical Roman antiquities, and whimsical Wild West artifacts. They all appear genuine—but Marchiori created them all in his on-site studio.

THE GRANDEUR OF THE STONE EDIFICE IS ALMOST PALPABLE. WELL over 200 feet long and three 18-foot stories high, the building dwarfs everything else around it. That is just how its original owner wanted it. Having seen the great châteaux of France, Finnish sea captain Gustav Niebaum wanted to equal or surpass them in his adopted home, the Napa Valley. In 1887 he launched Inglenook, one of Napa's earliest wineries. Visiting the property nearly a century later, film director Francis Ford Coppola determined to acquire it and make a statement of his own. The result is Niebaum-Coppola Estate Winery, where Niebaum's château-style architecture and snug, shiplike interior provide an ideal stage set for Coppola's flair for the dramatic. Immediately inside the winery's arched wooden doors is Niebaum's own tasting room,

Return to Glory

NAPA'S GLAMOROUS NIEBAUM-COPPOLA ESTATE

It's the perfect marriage of dramatic historic landmark and larger-than-life celebrity owner: Niebaum-Coppola winery, founded by a dashing sea-faring adventurer and owned today by Hollywood icon Francis Ford Coppola.

unchanged since he last used it. Nearby is a photo of the founder, one that conveys the forceful personality that made him a captain in his 20s and rich in his 30s. Everything else is a like a film directed by Coppola. Directly ahead, a grand, hand-crafted wooden staircase, designed by his longtime set designer Dean Tavoularis, brings you up to a dramatically lit, intimate chamber where you can all but touch the Godfather's desk, a Frederick Tucker automobile, and Coppola's Academy Award statuettes. A stained-glass window incorporates the laughing and crying faces that symbolize comedy and tragedy, and the display cases in the vaulted tasting room are steeply angled, like a raked theater stage that focuses your attention on the performance of Coppola's wines at the tasting bar. Beginning with simple reds and whites for the table, you eventually progress to Rubicon, an intensely flavored Cabernet Sauvignon inspired by Niebaum's original dream of making Napa Valley's wines the envy of the world.

Francis Ford Coppola restored
the estate of winery founder
Gustave Niebaum. He renovated
the château's interior and added
a park with a reflecting pool

THE *RUMBLEFISH* CHURNS THROUGH THE SWELLS FLOODING THE NARROW CHANNEL that connects Noyo Harbor to the cobalt-blue Pacific. Soon skipper Don Akin turns north along the coast, and the sea calms. It's a glorious winter day on the Mendocino Coast, and you face the warmth of the sun, still rising over the steep, forested hills that stand between you and Mendocino's vinelands. It's Crab & Wine Days, a ten-day January festival devoted to large-clawed crustaceans, and one of the featured attractions is a trip on a crab boat. Suddenly the engine throttles down and Akin points to a marker bobbing on the surface. It's time for the main event: pulling up the hatbox-shaped net below the marker and gathering in a clutch of squirming, scraping, Dungeness crabs. As the boat rocks, Akin and his assistant swing a winch out over the side, wind up the line attached to the net, swing the winch back amidships, and

Mendocino Gets Cracking

CRAB AND WINE ON THE PACIFIC COAST, MENDOCINO

Stirring scenery, superb B&Bs, and some of the world's freshest Dungeness crab—enjoy all this plus the salty sea spray so familiar to Pacific coast fishermen.

deposit the net's contents into a holding tank. They make it look easy, but you're happy to stand back from the thrumming cables, keening motors, and snapping claws. As soon as the crabs are aboard, they are measured and sexed. All females and immature males are back in the water in seconds, and then you're chugging on to the next marker. An hour or two later you disembark for lunch in Noyo, a cozy harbor with barking seals and clanking bells. A tangy young Riesling from Navarro Vineyards or crisp dry Sauvignon Blanc from Greenwood Ridge Winery makes a perfect complement to sweet, soft crab meat. You savor the combination with a fresh new perspective after watching your lunch come splashing up out of the sea, alive and kicking.

Relax in a swank dining room on the bluffs, or come as you are to a harborside dive. Whatever your pleasure, you can find it in Mendocino's restaurants, which connect you to the timeless abundance of the briny deep.

FINE BUBBLES RISE LIKE MINIATURE PEARLS. WINEMAKER MICHEL Salgues of Roederer Estate lifts his glass so the wine's pale gold gleams in the afternoon sun. "You cannot just drink a wine like this," he declares, with a charming French accent. "First you must get to know it a little bit." As the soft, tickly liquid slides across your tongue, a hawk soars above the oak-studded pastures down below. Michel pours another sample of his sparkling wine. This one is paler, but somehow its yeasty, melony flavors seem more vivid. He cocks a quizzical eyebrow. "A surprise, no?" He could be speaking about the entire Anderson Valley. It's one of California's most rural wine regions, yet it produces some of America's most refined wine: the kind with bubbles. You don't have to be French to love sparkling wine, or to make it your profession. At

Anderson Valley Sparklers

MENDOCINO: THE HOME OF AMERICA'S BEST BUBBLIES

Luscious grapes are harvested in Anderson Valley in early autumn, when warm, dry days are followed by cool, damp nights.

nearby Pacific Echo, winemaker "Tex" Sawyer's accent is all-American, as are his cowboy boots, blue jeans, and 1,000-watt smile. He even likens his vintage Brut Rosé to a freshly baked apple pie—but it would have to be one of the most sublime pies you've ever tasted. You take a glass outside to a café table on the white-trimmed terrace, where you linger over every sip. There's virtually nothing European about Handley Cellars, where an 18-foot wooden carving of a Papua New Guinea saltwater crocodile hangs over the door, and the tasting room features huge chunks of solid teak tree trunks carved into elephant chairs. Milla Handley's sparkling wines are as boldly original as the Indonesian, Mexican, and Indian folk art that fills the room, and she's known for holding back some of her best bottlings for later release. That means you could walk into the tasting room today and savor the captured, sparkling sunlight of a dozen summers past.

Sparkling wineries in Anderson Valley are close to their vineyards in a narrow, closed valley, ensuring that grapes are picked at optimum ripeness, crushed quickly, and pressed while their freshness is at its peak.

IMAGINE FLOATING IN WATER AS THE SOUND OF DISTANT, SOOTHING MUSIC ENVELOPS you. Strong, sensitive arms cradle your head and shoulders, then draw you gently backward. Your feet leave the bottom of the shallow pool and you allow yourself to be slowly pulled in a sweeping swirl that feels like flying. At first the sensation is strange. Then relaxation sets in: the body lengthens, the joints loosen, the breathing slows. You're outdoors, in a cloverleaf-shape Watsu massage pool at the Sonoma Mission Inn. This waterborne version of shiatsu massage uses your body's weightlessness to allow the practitioner to make adjustments in your musculature that are impossible on a massage table. The specially designed Watsu pools at this full-service spa resort are filled with warm mineral water that steams up from the earth on the resort grounds. And there's plenty of water to be found at the inn: at the

Liquid Bodies

AQUATIC HEALING AT SONOMA MISSION INN

The inn has a uniquely colorful history—after World War II the Navy used it to house sailors and marines who needed some R&R.

Roman-style bathhouse, illuminated by a rose-colored skylight, you can choose between bathing pools of different temperatures, slip into a steam bath, or take a cool shower. Unwind, later, in the spa's main lounge—nestle into an overstuffed armchair in front of a crackling fire and sip a cup of tea or lime-scented mineral water. You can easily fill a day at the spa with a long massage, a grape-seed body polish, some sunbathing by the outdoor pool (it's warm even in winter), and an al fresco lunch. If that's a bit too restful for you, simply add in visits to wineries, galleries, and boutiques, a hike in the hills nearby, or a round on the inn's own verdant, redwood-shaded golf course. On your return you'll be restored with creative spa cuisine—a citrus and celery-root salad with spicy pecans, clay oven—roasted prawns, or medallions of ostrich.

AROUND A PRIVATE VERANDA IN A LEAFY, SUNLIT WOOD, ALL IS STILL except for occasional birdsong. Then the sound—*thwick!*—of a golf club striking a golf ball squarely on the sweet spot. Far below, through the leaves, you can see an undulating green where a golf ball lands, rolls, and stops a foot from the cup. A congratulatory shout floats up through the trees at Napa Valley's Meadowood Resort. Although just minutes from the vineyards, it feels a world away in its secluded valley. At Meadowood you can play like a kid, be pampered like a queen, and dine like a king without ever getting into your car. As you stroll down a shady lane, you might pick up the sounds of other pleasures. *Thock!* A wooden mallet hammers a croquet ball on one of the immaculate championship courts. *Thung!* A tennis player slams an overhead for

Summer Camp for Adults

SYBARITIC SPLENDOR AT MEADOWOOD RESORT, NAPA

Nature itself seems to relax and glow with good health at Meadowood, a hidden valley rimmed with oak woodlands where the sun is never too hot and the wind is always a breeze.

a winner. Through the trees you can hear swimmers splash in a spa-side pool and glasses clink on a shady terrace. Along your route are posh rooms, suites, and cottages artfully arrayed in hillside groves. Guests spend little time in their rooms, however. Meadowood is a major cultural resource for the Napa Valley—concerts, classes, and literary lunches are held here throughout the year. In the spa, where you sign in for a mid-afternoon massage, you overhear members discussing the season's grape harvest. You're not the only eavesdropper—Meadowood is a magnet for connoisseurs and vintners from around the world, and the Wine Center hosts tasting games, seminars, and winery tours. The resort is also home to the famed Napa Valley Wine Auction—a summer event in which some enthusiasts bid as high as $100,000 for a single bottle of wine.

For many Napa vintners, Meadowood is a home away from home, so you'll see them mixing easily with other members, old friends, and new acquaintances on the golf course, tennis courts, and croquet courts.

THE WINDING ROAD THROUGH THE VINEYARDS STRAIGHTENS AND broadens into a wide boulevard as it approaches the town of Sonoma, the California wine country's most historic city. It has been this way since the 1820s, when Spanish missionaries completed El Camino Real—the Royal Road—from Mexico to northern California. The final stop then and now: Mission San Francisco Solano de Sonoma, built by Franciscan friars to bring their culture and religion to indigenous tribes. A walk through the austere, wood-beamed chapel and workshops reveals how simple life was then, before Mexican General Mariano Vallejo marched in and took over in 1834. He turned the end of El Camino Real into an 8-acre plaza and used it as the parade ground for his troops. Today this lively town square doubles as Sonoma State Historic Park. Under

Wine Country Epicenter

THE 19TH-CENTURY MISSION TOWN OF SONOMA

Sonoma's central plaza preserves intriguing, historic monuments from every era of its colorful past, beginning with its founding by Franciscan missionaries in the 1820s.

the plaza's tall trees, schoolchildren draw pictures of the venerable town hall, artists hawk their creations in outdoor exhibits, and picnickers pop the corks on bottles of Sonoma Zinfandel. The plaza is ringed with adobe buildings that house exhibits, shops, restaurants, and hotels. Their wisteria-draped 19th-century balconies once shaded the bandit Joaquin Murietta, the frontiersman Kit Carson, and a young army captain named Ulysses S. Grant. These are just a few of the many adventurers, heroes, and desperadoes who populated Sonoma, and you can recapture their spirit in the Toscano Hotel. This landmark is so well preserved that it seems as if a card game has been suddenly interrupted, perhaps by news of another gold strike—the whisky glasses are still on the table, and the piano is still playing.

AT ANY HOUR OF THE DAY, A GASTRONOMIC INDULGENCE AWAITS YOU IN the Napa Valley hamlet of Yountville. In the morning, valley vintners and restaurateurs flock to Gordon's Café and Wine Bar at the quiet north end of town, where they sit at communal tables to consume Sally Gordon's fresh baked goods, zesty omelettes, and eye-opening espresso. Before the clock strikes noon, the midday meal gets under way all around town. At Domaine Chandon, long al fresco lunches unfold on the terrace overlooking the garden, and diners can select one of the winery's dozen different sparklers with each new course. Downtown, savvy late lunchers arrive at Bistro Jeanty for a mid-afternoon intermezzo, when the crowds have thinned, the *pommes frites* are at their crispest, and there's no competition for Phillipe Jeanty's battle-scarred foosball table on the trellis-

Bring Your Appetite

TOP TABLES IN YOUNTVILLE, NAPA VALLEY

The ruggedly chic Vintage 1870, an old winery complex of vine-covered brick buildings, now houses dainty boutiques and food stores with every imaginable flavor—sweet plump fruit, sharp cheeses, smoky meats.

shaded patio. The other French place in town, Bouchon, is just a few doors away. Famed chef Thomas Keller launched Bouchon because he wanted a simpler alternative to the lavish menus he devises daily for his first restaurant, The French Laundry, nearby. One of the best times at Bouchon begins at five-thirty in summer, when the western sun slants through the windows and the raw bar is freshly stocked with succulent oysters and mussels. An hour later, the elegant, high-ceilinged room fills with high-spirited diners served by fast-moving, white-aproned waiters. For a less boisterous experience, take a table at Brix—the sous chefs wield flashing knives and sizzling sauté pans in the warmly lit open kitchen—and marvel at chef Michael Patton's spicy ahi tuna futomaki roll or Chilean sea bass saltimbocca on polenta with white truffle and Parmesan. Outside, on the terrace, look out into fragrant organic gardens surrounded by vineyards, and watch the sun disappear into the Mayacamas Mountains to the west.

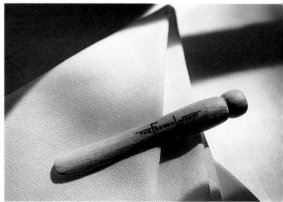

The justly famous French Laundry is only the best-known restaurant in Yountville, which has become a boomtown for fancy food—Old World Italian and French country-rustic cooking, well-spiced East-West fusion, and famously mouthwatering California cuisine.

71

Savor the bold, bright flavor and color of just-boiled lobster dripping with golden butter, or the meaty crab and oysters freshly shucked, or the always-seductive staple of steak frites and succulent onion soup.

Grapes into Wine

Winegrowers and winemakers operate on different but interrelated calendars. The two share a peak in autumn, when grapes are picked and winemaking begins.

SEASONS OF THE VINE

Premium wine grapes are specialized varieties that have been cultivated and refined for millennia. The rugged, geologically complex terrain of northern California offers winegrowers an extremely wide range of soil types and microclimates, which means they can grow an extraordinary range of varieties with enviable consistency year after year. Grapes are planted using varying systems of spacing, trellising, and irrigation, all aimed at producing the highest-quality fruit.

In late fall, after the grapes are harvested, the vines lose their leaves and go dormant for the winter. During this time, winegrowers prune each vine back to its most productive branches. New buds pop out in March, followed six to twelve weeks later by flowering and pollination. By June, small bunches of tiny green grapes appear, giving vintners a sense of the size of the crop to come.

In August, the grapes begin to change color. White wine grapes (such as Chardonnay and Sauvignon Blanc) turn yellow and gold. Red wine grapes (such as Cabernet Sauvignon, Merlot, Pinot Noir, and Zinfandel) darken further until they are red, purple, dark blue, or even black. In late August or early September, winemakers walk the vineyards, seeking the moment when the grapes contain optimum levels of sugar and acid—sugars carry flavor and ferment into alcohol, while acids confer structure and texture. For the next two months or more, as the grapes reach maturity, pickers bring them in acre by acre, vineyard by vineyard.

STAGES OF WINE

When grapes arrive at the winery, usually in half-ton bins, they are first crushed gently to break open the fruit. Red wine grapes are left in this condition in large tanks for up to several weeks, so that the clear juice inside the grapes can soak up color and additional acidity from the skins. In contrast, juice destined to become white wine is pressed off the skins almost immediately after crushing. This difference in skin contact accounts for many differences between red and white wine, including those of color, texture, and longevity.

Both red and white wine are fermented in stainless steel tanks or, less frequently, in wooden barrels.

Yeasts, which are either naturally present or added by winemakers, consume the sugar in the juice and convert it to alcohol. During this fermentation, wine is segregated by grape variety and by vineyard, sometimes even by blocks within the vineyard. When fermentation is complete, the different lots of wine are set aside to age. For white wines, this process may entail six months in stainless steel. For reds, it can mean two years in expensive oak barrels.

Before bottling, the various wines are blended together, usually in time-honored combinations such as Sauvignon Blanc and Semillon, or Zinfandel and Petite Sirah. Occasionally a single grape variety from a single vineyard delivers a complete wine on its own. Most of the time, however, winemakers blend several grape varieties from more than one vineyard to create the finished wine.

All the Details

The California wine country covered in this book includes the Napa Valley, the three major wine valleys of Sonoma County, and the Anderson Valley and coastal environs of Mendocino County. All these areas are north of San Francisco. Most visitors from outside northern California fly into the San Francisco Bay area—either San Francisco International or Oakland International airport—and rent a car. San Francisco is a bit more convenient to Sonoma and Mendocino, but Oakland has the edge for Napa. If it's not rush hour, it should take you 1½ to 2 hours to reach Napa destinations, 75 minutes to 2½ hours to reach Sonoma destinations, and 3 to 4 hours to reach Mendocino destinations. Subtract 45 minutes if you are starting out from San Francisco, not the airports.

You can mix multiple escapes in one short visit, but remember that moving between the wine valleys takes time. On summer weekends it can take almost an hour to get from the north end of Napa Valley down to the city of Napa. On any day the western end of Russian River Valley in Sonoma County is over an hour by car from the city of Sonoma.

There's no bad time of year to visit, as northern California weather can be warm and sunny in December or cold and foggy in July. The one constant is that rain rarely falls from April to November. Bring layers of clothing, comfortable walking shoes, and a hat for the sun.

Even if you rent your own car, consider renting a limousine or taking a tour for a day or half-day of wine-tasting (your inn or hotel can arrange it). You'll see more scenery, taste more wine, and enjoy your companions more if you don't have to navigate unfamiliar country roads under the effects of alcohol. If you buy wine, arrange to have it shipped home—airlines have become stricter about shipping wine onboard their aircraft.

For information on visiting Napa Valley, contact the Napa Valley Conference & Visitor Bureau (1310 Napa Town Center, Napa 94559, tel. 707/226–7459, www.napavalley.com). For Sonoma County, use the resources given for each chapter or visit www.gosonoma.com for a listing of visitor bureaus throughout the county. For Mendocino, contact the Mendocino County Alliance (525 S. Main St., Suite E, Ukiah 95482, tel. 707/462–7417 or 866/466–3636, fax 707/468–9887, www.gomendo.com).

MENDOCINO

Like its sister to the south, Sonoma, Mendocino County is home to a variety of wine regions and is heavily influenced by the nearby Pacific Ocean. Its best-known wine valley is Anderson Valley (4F–5G), a long narrow strip of vineyards and orchards seemingly dropped whole into the rugged coastal mountains that separate Alexander Valley and Dry Creek Valleys (7I–10J) from the ocean. The scenic, two-lane Highway 128 that traverses Anderson Valley first passes through Yorkville Highlands, an officially designated wine region in its own right. The pull of Mendocino village (2D), an historic 19th-century harbor town, keeps tourists flowing through Yorkville Highlands and Anderson Valley and on to the water's edge. The climate, however, caused winemakers to stop well short of the coast, so they could take advantage of ideal growing conditions: hot, dry days combined with foggy mornings and cool evenings. This enables winemakers to produce the sparkling wine that many critics consider America's greatest challenge to true French Champagne.

THE APPLE FARM, ANDERSON VALLEY, MENDOCINO *(4G)*
Orchard Idyll, p. 40

Before it became vineland, Anderson Valley was prime orchard country. At the 34-acre Apple Farm you return to the orchard life of yesteryear. Your hosts are Sally and Don

Schmitt and Karen and Tim Bates (Karen is Sally and Don's daughter). They all live on the farm, producing organically grown heirloom apples, juices, chutneys, and other products. During summer and fall you can walk up to the open barn and sample these products yourself. To take something with you, simply leave your money in the basket on the counter: at the Apple Farm, trusting strangers is still in fashion. Your private cottage floats amid the apple trees, a short walk past roses and herb beds from the big country kitchen where Sally and Karen prepare breakfast and teach country cooking classes. If you'd like to prepare your own lunch or dinner in the kitchen, be sure to ask.

CONTACT: The Apple Farm, 18501 Greenwood Rd., Philo 95482, tel. 707/895–2461. Three cottages in the orchard. Each has a queen-size bed with colorful cotton-and-down bedding, gas log hearthstone stove, high ceilings, screened doors and porch, outdoor seating on porch, and ceiling fan. Bathrooms are big; one cottage has a claw-foot tub and outdoor shower; others have oversized showers. "Room with a View," perched above the Apple Farm's dining room, overlooks the orchard and redwoods. It has lots of large windows, a queen-size bed, and a large tile shower. $175 nightly. No TV or phones.

DISTANCES: 115 mi from San Francisco. Take U.S. 101 north to California's Highway 128 west.

OPTIONS: Just across the Navarro River from the Apple Farm is **Hendy Woods State Park** (4G): 800 acres of forest rising from the river toward the ridge. Giant old-growth redwoods stand just inside the park's entrance—leave the park road as soon as you find a footpath below and to the left, skirting the boundary fence. Just before the park's entrance on the opposite side of the road is the path down to the local swimming hole. When the weather's hot, locals of all ages cool off under the high bridge. A short drive farther along the Philo-Greenwood road takes you to the 4-mi driveway of **Highland Lodge,** a dude ranch that leads horseback rides overlooking the valley and vineyards below. A few miles up the valley, the town of Boonville (5G) is home to the **Mendocino County Fair and Apple Show** each September and numerous other events throughout the year (tel. 707/489–3953, www.boonville.org).

To get to wineries, simply head down Highway 128 in either direction. Standouts include **Greenwood Ridge Vineyards** (tel. 707/895−2002), **Handley Cellars** (tel. 707/895−3876), **Navarro Vineyards** (tel. 707/895−3686), **Pacific Echo** (tel. 707/895−2065), **Roederer Estate** (tel. 707/895−2288), and **Yorkville Cellars** (tel. 707/894−9177).

CRAB AND WINE ON THE PACIFIC COAST, MENDOCINO *(2D)*
Mendocino Gets Cracking, p. 52

The 10-day Crab and Wine Days festival brackets the last weekend in January and the first weekend in February, when locals are eager to welcome off-season visitors. (This period includes Superbowl weekend, but don't worry; there are events designed around watching the game on big-screen TVs.) Mendocino's winter skies can be piercingly clear or dramatically stormy, so check the weather report if you're determined to get out on a crab boat. If the boats are staying in the harbor, there's still plenty to do: museum visits, cooking demonstrations, and art exhibits. No matter what the weather report says, bring layers and a hat wherever you go. The Mendocino coast is heaven if you're a bed-and-breakfast lover; expect everything from rustic 1800s cottages to elegant modern inns. Many of the area's abundant fine restaurants participate in the festival. The most picturesque of the larger towns is Mendocino village; stop in for at least a few hours for a leisurely stroll past shop windows and along the whale-watching bluffs.

CONTACT: Mendocino County Alliance, 525 S. Main St., Suite E, Ukiah 95482, tel. 707/462−7417 or 866/466−3636, www.gomendo.com.

LODGING: The coziest location for crab enthusiasts is the **Lodge at Noyo River,** which, perched directly above the snug harbor, has commanding views. Get a room or suite in the main house. 500 Casa Del Noyo Dr., Ft. Bragg 95437, tel. 707/964−8045, 800/628−5642, www.noyolodge.com. 16 rooms with harbor views, garden, and full breakfast. From $99. The most convenient lodging for families and festival events is the **Little River Inn,** which has a restaurant, tennis courts, and golf course, and sponsors daytime and evening festival activities.

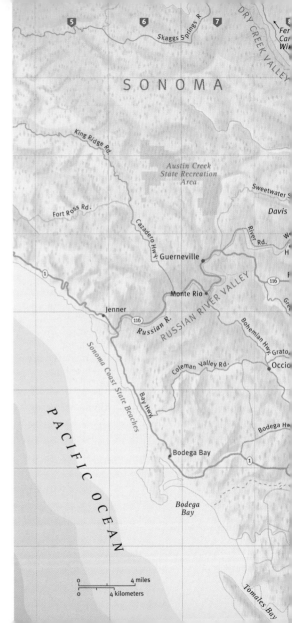

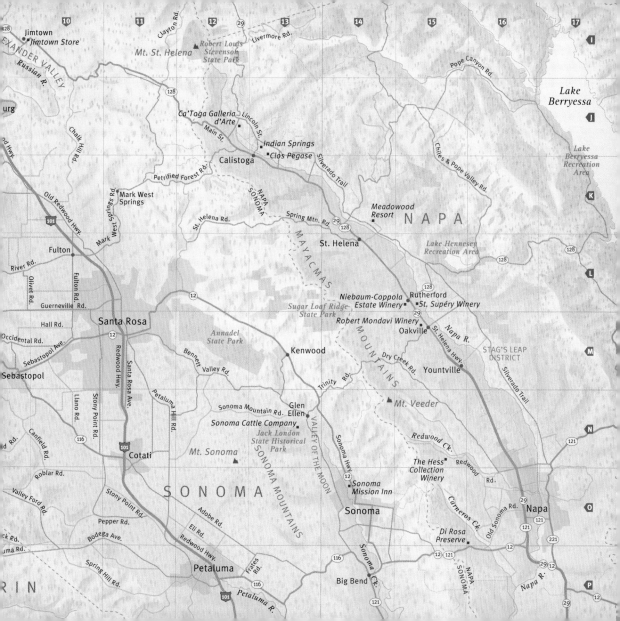

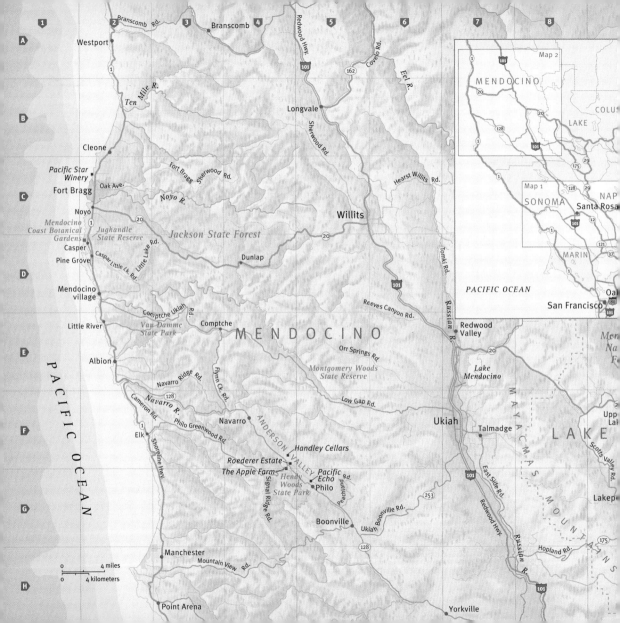

Little River, California 95456, tel. 707/937—5942 or 888/466—5683, www.littleriverinn.com. 67 rooms with ocean views; some also have fireplaces and hot tubs. From $135.

OPTIONS: Wineries are located all along Highway 128 in Anderson Valley, the main route to the Mendocino Coast from U.S. 101. Standouts include **Greenwood Ridge, Handley Cellars** (4F), **Navarro, Roederer Estate** (4F), **Pacific Echo** (5G), and **Yorkville Cellars**. Local restaurants don't mind opening the wine you bring if you don't mind paying the corkage. If you're not already booked into a winemaker dinner as part of the festival, check out **Albion River Inn** (3790 Hwy. 1, Albion, tel. 707/937—1919) or **Ledford House** (3000 N. Hwy. 1, Albion, tel. 707/937—0282), and **955 Ukiah** (955 Ukiah St., tel. 707/937—1955), **Cafe Beaujolais** (961 Ukiah St., tel. 707/937—5614), **MacCallum House** (45020 Albion St., tel. 707/937—5763), or **Moosse Cafe** (390 Kasten St., tel. 707/937—4323) in Mendocino village. It's also fun to hit the seafood dives down in the harbor towns. The **Skunk Train,** an old narrow-gauge railroad that winds through the forests from the coast inland to Willits (5–6C), is a favorite with train fans of all ages (California Western Railroad Depot, beginning of Laurel St., Ft. Bragg, tel. 707/964—6371). If the whales are running, the best place to spot them is from the bluffs of **Mendocino Headlands State Park,** just a short stroll from Mendocino village (visitor center at 735 Main St., tel. 707/937—5397).

MENDOCINO: THE HOME OF AMERICA'S BEST BUBBLIES (4F–5G)
Anderson Valley Sparklers, p. 56

Twenty years ago a famed French Champagne house named Roederer built its American outpost in Mendocino's rustic Anderson Valley. At that time conventional wisdom held that only Sonoma and Napa could produce premium sparkling wine. Winemaker Michel Salgues proved them wrong, and before long local vintners John Scharffenberger and Milla Handley joined him in making outstanding bubbly. (Most American producers bow to the French insistence that only their sparkling wine can be called Champagne.) Another top Champagne house, Veuve Clicquot, bought Scharffenberger's winery, changed the name to Pacific Echo (5G), and expanded its production. Today, on a visit to Anderson Valley you can explore three distinct and representative personalities in American sparkling wine: the French restraint of Roederer Estate, the outspoken, individualistic personality of Handley Cellars, and the polished yet assertive style of Pacific Echo. All three are within a few miles of each other in or near the town of Philo.

CONTACT: Handley Cellars (4F), 3151 Hwy. 128, 6 mi northwest of Philo, tel. 707/895—3151. Tasting room open 11—6 in summer, 11—5 in winter; tours by appointment. Sparkling and still wines to taste and purchase, and a garden courtyard for picnics; art, artifacts, and jewelry for sale in the tasting room. **Pacific Echo** (5G), 8501 Hwy. 128, Philo, tel. 707/895—2065. Tasting room open 11—5; tours by appointment. Sparkling and still wines to taste and purchase; flower garden, shaded lawn and terrace courtyard for picnics; fine art on exhibit and for sale in the tasting room. **Roederer Estate** (4F), 4501 Hwy. 128, 5 mi northwest of Philo, tel. 707/895—2288; tasting room open 11—5; tours by appointment. Sparkling and still wines to taste and purchase; comfortable table seating in the elegant tasting room overlooking the valley.

DISTANCES: 110 to 115 mi from San Francisco. Take U.S. 101 north to Hwy. 128 west.

LODGING: The **Boonville Hotel** is not your average country roadhouse. The artistic atmosphere and off-center attitude stem from owner Johnny Schmitt, who designed the guest rooms and runs the restaurant kitchen. Hwy. 128 at Lambert La., Box 326, Boonville 95415, tel. 707/895—2210, www.boonvillehotel.com. The 10 rooms are all different, with furnishings and decoration by local artisans. Rooms range from a small double with a deck to good-sized suites with private entrances, screened porches, and room for pets. All rooms have private baths. None has a TV or phone. From $85. The restaurant at the Boonville Hotel is Anderson Valley's top dining room, pushed not by local competition but pulled by Schmitt's restless intelligence and the surprisingly sophisticated local palates. The **Anderson Creek Inn** (tel. 800/552—6202, www.andersoncreekinn.com) and **Philo Pottery Inn** (tel. 707/895—3069, www.philopotteryinn.com) are recommended for those who prefer a B&B experience.

OPTIONS: Boonville (5G) is spread out for 2 mi along Highway 128, with most establishments worth visiting within a short walk of the Boonville Hotel. Just across the road is the **Boonville Tasting Room,** shared by Claudia Springs Winery, Eagle Point Ranch Winery, and Rayes Hill Winery. Right next door is the **Boonville General Store,** where the merchandise and prices add an urban edge to Boonville's decidedly small-town charm. **Café Glad** (tel. 707/895—3038, Mon.–Sat. 8—3) is where locals go for coffee and morning pastry, and **Lauren's** (tel. 707/895—3869, Tues.–Sat. 5 pm—9 pm) is where they go for dinner. You should do the same if the Boonville Hotel is closed, full, or where you ate last night. Just outside town is one of America's top microbreweries, **Anderson Valley Brewing Company** (17700 Hwy. 253, at Hwy. 128, tel. 707/895—BEER), with tours daily at 1:30 and 4; reservations recommended. Two miles northwest of the Boonville Hotel on the southwest side of Highway 128 is the **Anderson Valley Historical Society Museum** (tel. 707/895—3207), which is open on weekends only but is worth a visit for its window on a past that seems not so distant in this Arcadian valley. Boonville is the home of the **Mendocino County Fair and Apple Show** (tel. 707/489—3953, www.boonville.org) each September and of other enjoyable events throughout the year. When you've visited the three sparkling wineries, your top choices among the still wineries are **Christine Woods Winery** (tel. 707/895—2115), **Greenwood Ridge Vineyards** (tel. 707/895—2002), **Husch Vineyards** (tel. 707/895—3216), **Navarro Vineyards** (tel. 707/895—3686), and **Yorkville Cellars** (tel. 707/894—9177).

A MEETING OF MUSIC, FOOD, AND WINE IN MENDOCINO (2C–D)
Winesong!, p. 26

Winesong! takes place on the second Saturday in September, in the Mendocino Coast Botanical Gardens along the Pacific Coast Highway (U.S. 1) in Ft. Bragg (2C). The event opens with a relaxed, musical wine and food tasting in the redwood forest at the heart of the gardens. Mendocino County's many wineries are well represented, and an increasing number of leading wineries from Napa and Sonoma participate as well. Restaurants, bakeries, and other food purveyors attend, along with the wineries, so you can mix and match tastes and flavors in countless combinations. The wine auction includes as many as 300 lots, ranging from single bottles of wine to a winery dinner for eight or a lavish, all-expense-paid trip for two to the Caribbean. There is also a silent auction in an adjoining tent, where connoisseurs hunt for exceptional deals. Dress warmly—the Pacific Ocean is just ½ mi away, so it can be breezy.

CONTACT: Winesong!, 700 River Dr., Fort Bragg 95437, tel. 707/961—4688, www.winesong.org. Auction Reserve ticketholders are guaranteed table seating for the auction and early admission to the pre-auction tasting in the botanical gardens.

DISTANCES: 150 mi north of San Francisco. The most direct route is U.S. 101 north to Highway 128 west to U.S. 1 north. Eight mi north of Mendocino village, 2 mi south of downtown Ft. Bragg (2C).

LODGING: The town of Mendocino is one of America's most scenic coastal villages. For years it stood in for the fictitious New England town of Cabot Cove on the popular TV series "Murder, She Wrote." Book ahead so you can stay in the historic district, where the original Victorian houses must be maintained with painstaking authenticity. **C. O. Packard House** is one of Mendocino's finest restorations on the outside and one of its most engaging B&Bs on the inside. Owners Maria and Daniel Levin seem to be masters of everything related to innkeeping, from designing and decorating wonderful rooms to cooking and serving fantastic breakfasts. 45170 Little Lake Rd., Mendocino 95460, tel. 707/937—2677 or 888/453—2677, fax 707/937—1323, www.packardhouse.com. 7 sumptuous rooms, all with private bath, TV/VCR, and other amenities. From $145. The most historic B&B stay is at **John Dougherty House,** named for its original owner, a 19th-century Mendocino sea captain who built the house to look out over the rocky cove where his boat would lie at anchor. 71 Ukiah St., Mendocino 95460, tel. 707/937—5266 or 800/486—2104, www.johndoughertyhouse.com. Rooms in the original house feature period furniture and antique art, and an heirloom flower garden beckons in back. 8 rooms, all with private bath and wood-burning fireplace. From $105.

OPTIONS: The only winery in the area, **Pacific Star** (2C), should be at the top of your list for adventuring on the Mendocino Coast. The winery and tasting room overlook crashing waves 12 mi north of Ft. Bragg. 3000 N. Hwy. 1, Ft. Bragg, tel. 707/964—1155, www.pacificstarwinery.com. Proprietor Sally Ottoson is a native of the Mendocino Coast, a talented winemaker, and a gracious hostess. Call ahead for a tasting appointment before or after Winesong! (she will be attending the event and pouring her wines before the auction that day). The entire town of Mendocino is an attraction on its own, as it occupies a bluff thrust out into the Pacific Ocean. There are shops and galleries on every commercial street, historic buildings everywhere, and the water's edge is just a short stroll from the center of town. The **Kelley House Museum** (45007 Albion St., tel. 707/937—5791), which has exhibits that depict the history of Mendocino, is a good place to start your day. For a memorable outdoor excursion, visit **Jughandle State Reserve** (2D) and take the nature walk that leads up through five different coastal microclimates to a rare pygmy forest. Five mi north of Mendocino on U.S. 1, parking on the west side of the highway. More options in Mendocino and along the coast are included in "Mendocino Gets Cracking."

NAPA

Napa Valley is a long crescent moon with its northern tip at Calistoga (13J–K) and its southern tip near San Francisco Bay. Mountains ranging up to 2,700 feet line both sides of the valley, and the Napa River courses through its length. The city of Napa (16N–17P) is the valley's largest municipality, and its star is definitely ascendant, as Robert and Margrit Mondavi are leading a cultural and culinary renaissance downtown. Farther "up valley," as locals say, are three smaller towns: Yountville (15–16M), Oakville (15M), and Rutherford (15L). All lie along the major artery, Highway 29 (also known as St. Helena Highway), and are surrounded by famous vineyards, including those of Mondavi, Beaulieu, and Niebaum-Coppola. In all, there are more than 250 wineries in the Napa River watershed. Continuing north on 29

brings you to St. Helena (14L), a small town that is home to historic wineries (such as Beringer and Krug) as well as encroaching boutiques (such as Wilkes-Bashford). Finally there is Calistoga (13J–K), the original 19th-century magnet that drew San Franciscans up the valley to luxuriate in the natural hot springs. In that regard, at least, little has changed.

ART AMONG THE VINES IN THE NAPA VALLEY
(12J–16P)
The Eyes Have It, p. 34

The Napa Valley is home to three extraordinary art collections on permanent public display, and you can visit them all in a long day or leisurely weekend. The di Rosa Preserve (16O) is in the Carneros winegrowing district, between San Francisco and Napa. The art is displayed in a 100-year-old former winery, new galleries, and 200 acres of meadows and gardens maintained as a nature preserve. The Hess Collection (15N) is a century-old winery on Mt. Veeder, above and to the west of the valley floor. The art collection occupies a space that resembles a chic urban museum, with its own curator and gallery director. Clos Pegase (13J), toward the north end of the valley near Calistoga, is also a large, working winery with an impressive collection, but the art is smoothly integrated into the buildings and grounds. Plan to visit on the third Saturday of the month, when owner Jan Shrem gives his entertaining, informative presentation titled "A Bacchanalian History of Wine Seen Through 4,000 Years of Art."

CONTACT: Clos Pegase, 1060 Dunaweal La., Calistoga 94515, tel. 707/942—4981, fax 707/942—4993, www.clospegase.com. Open daily 10:30—5. Free tours conducted daily at 11 and 2. Wine tasting $3. The **di Rosa Preserve,** 5200 Carneros Hwy. (Hwy. 121), Napa 94559, tel. 707/226—5991, www.dirosapreserve.org. Open by reservation only. Tours cost $12. **Hess Collection Winery,** 4411 Redwood Rd., Napa 94558, tel. 707/255—1144, www.hesscollection.com. Open daily 10—4. Self-guided winery tour is free. Wine tasting $3.

DISTANCES: The di Rosa Preserve, the Hess Collection, and Clos

Pegase are, respectively, 35 mi, 50 mi, and 60 mi from San Francisco.

OPTIONS: You'll find art almost everywhere in the Napa Valley if you know where to look. In downtown Napa, **Copia** (707/259-1600 or 888/512-6742, www.copia.org, closed Tuesday and Wednesday) offers contemporary art, installations, and exhibits focusing on interrelations among wine, food, and the arts. **Robert Mondavi Winery** (7801 St. Helena Hwy., Oakville, tel. 707/ 259—9463) and **St. Supéry Winery** (8440 St. Helena Hwy., Rutherford, tel. 800/942—0809) maintain permanent galleries that host changing exhibits, and many other wineries have art on the walls in their tasting rooms. If you visit **Auberge du Soleil** (180 Rutherford Hill Rd., Rutherford, tel. 707/964—1211) for lunch, look for the outdoor sculpture garden, hidden away at the bottom of the hill below the cottage terraces. There are outstanding commercial galleries in the towns of Yountville, St. Helena, and Calistoga, including **Art on Main** (359 Main St., St. Helena, tel. 707/963—3350), **Ca'Toga Galleria d'Arte** (1206 Cedar St., Calistoga, tel. 707/942—3900; *see* "Master of Illusion"), **Images Fine Art** (6540 Washington St., Yountville, tel. 707/944—0404), and **Lee Youngman Galleries** (1316 Lincoln Ave. Calistoga, tel. 707/942—0585). A few successful artists have opened their own galleries in the Napa Valley over the years, and in some you will still find the artists at work. Eric Christensen (**The Working Studio,** 6525 Washington St., Yountville, tel. 707/945—0650) paints brightly colored, densely layered watercolor still lifes. Jessel Miller (**Jessel Gallery,** 1019 Atlas Peak Rd., Napa, tel. 707/257—2350) is a prolific worker in a variety of mediums, and an enthusiastic booster of all things artistic in the Napa Valley.

BALLOONING OVER NAPA VALLEY *(15–16M)*
Dawn Flight, p. 8

Expect to arrive at your launch point before daylight, which during the long days of early summer means 5:30 am. At other times of the year you check in an hour or more later. Before your arrival you specify the size of balloon you want, depending on the number in your party. Napa Valley Aloft sends its balloons skyward from the parking lots of the Vintage 1870

shopping complex in centrally located Yountville. After a cup of coffee and a pre-flight briefing, you head outside to watch seasoned ground crews inflate the day's balloons, and soon get airborne. When you come down, a chase crew drives up to deflate the balloon, pack it up, and take you back to a sumptuous Champagne breakfast.

CONTACT: Napa Valley Aloft, Vintage 1870, 6525 Washington St., Box 2290, Yountville 94599, tel. 707/944—8638 or 800/627—2759, fax 707/944—4406, www.napavalleyaloft.com. Napa Valley Aloft also does business as Above the West Ballooning, Adventures Aloft, and Balloon Aviation of Napa Valley. The company picks up passengers at various points in Napa Valley (and San Francisco), so you can leave your car behind if you like. From $185 per person.

DISTANCES: 55 mi from San Francisco, 9 mi from downtown Napa, 12 mi from St. Helena.

LODGING: The Oak Knoll Inn offers a gracious wine-country experience, with vineyards around the inn and balloons drifting overhead in the early morning. 2200 E. Oak Knoll Ave., Napa 94558, tel. 707/255—2200, fax 707/225—2296, www.oakknollinn.com. Each of the four large, well-appointed rooms has a fireplace, private bath, and separate entrance. You can also join others at the inn's afternoon wine tastings or on tailored itineraries arranged by proprietress Barbara Passino, an articulate, enthusiastic ambassador for the wine country. Shared amenities include a swimming pool, a Jacuzzi, a library, and a feast of a breakfast each morning. Book well ahead if you can, but don't be afraid to call at the last minute. From $285.

OPTIONS: Ballooning is available year-round in Napa Valley, which goes out of its way to accommodate the occasional surprise landing in someone's backyard. If you prefer to balloon in the more compact valleys of Sonoma County, contact **Aerostat Adventures** in Healdsburg (9J) (tel. 800/579—0183) or **Up & Away Ballooning** in Windsor (9K) (tel. 800/711—2998) to check on dates and availability. Ballooning is an activity that gets you up quite early and feeds you a sizable breakfast rather late, so you may want to book dinner on the early side and skip lunch. See "Bring Your Appetite" for excellent restaurant choices in Yountville. Between ballooning and dinner—if you don't need

a nap—you can visit wineries you saw from the air. **Domaine Chandon** (tel. 707/944—8844, www.chandon-usa.com) is one of the larger winemaking facilities near Yountville, and it offers winery tours and tastings of premium sparkling wine year-round. **Stags Leap** (tel. 707/255—1720, www.stagsleapdistrict.com) is a nearby wine district known for its Cabernet Sauvignon. Oakville and Rutherford, with numerous destination wineries, are just a few miles up the highway, so you won't have to stray too far to get the full sense of Napa's country.

INDIAN SPRINGS RESORT, CALISTOGA *(13J)*
Steam Heat, p. 12

With its broad lawns, tall palms, and curving drive, the resort takes you back to the days when Sam Brannan, California's first gold-rush millionaire, had big plans for his adopted state. At the time, America's best-known resort was at Saratoga, in New York. Legend has it that one inebriated night Brannan was trying to say "the Saratoga of California" and came out with "Calistoga of Sarifornia." When you want to rejoin the 21st century, it's just a short walk to downtown Calistoga, with its up-to-the-minute collection of restaurants, galleries, and shops.

CONTACT: Indian Springs, 1712 Lincoln Ave., Calistoga 94515, tel. 707/942—4913, fax 707/942—4919, www.indianspring scalistoga.com.

DISTANCES: Calistoga is at the far northern end of Napa Valley, 30 minutes or more from the town of Napa on busy weekends and 72 mi from San Francisco. Indian Springs is within easy walking distance of the center of town.

LODGING: Accommodations at Indian Springs consist of 18 restored 1940s bungalows with old-fashioned covered porches, hammocks under the trees, and croquet wickets on the lawns. Ask for a barbecue grill if all this Americana moves you to cook out in the backyard (you'll also have a small but functional kitchen). Sizes range from cozy studio-style cottages to a three-bedroom, two-bathroom house perfect for families. Fireplaces, TV, air conditioning, down comforters, and terry-cloth robes are among the amenities that will make you feel right at home. If you need a phone, bring your own. From $215.

OPTIONS: Indian Springs offers a range of spa packages for overnight visitors and day trippers. If you have time, combine your one-hour mud bath treatment (which includes a hot soak, steam room, and blanket wrap) with a massage. To see what Calistoga's founder Sam Brannan built before his dream foundered, don't miss the **Sharpsteen Museum** (1311 Washington St., 1 block north of Lincoln, tel. 707/942—5911) and its 32-foot diorama of Brannan's original resort. Calistoga is home to some of Napa's most colorful local events, including the Napa County Fair, art shows, horse shows, history festivals, and, in December, a lighted tractor parade. Contact the Chamber of Commerce (The Depot, Lincoln Ave., tel. 707/942—6333) for information on all these and more. Another kind of color is at work at artist Carlo Marchiori's Ca' Toga (*see* "Master of Illusion"). Dining in Calistoga is a matter of mood. You can walk to a dozen great places to eat, so check them out during the day and then match your mood in the evening. You're likely to wind up at one of the following: **All Seasons Cafe & Wine Shop** (1400 Lincoln Ave., tel. 707/942—9111), **Brannan's Grill** (1374 Lincoln Ave., tel. 707/942—2233), **Catahoula Restaurant & Saloon** (1457 Lincoln Ave., tel. 707/942—2275), and **Wappo Bar & Bistro** (1226 Washington St., tel. 707/942—4712).

SYBARITIC SPLENDOR AT MEADOWOOD RESORT *(14K)*
Summer Camp for Adults, p. 62

Meadowood offers 24 rooms, 47 suites, and seven cottages scattered about a private 250-acre valley that feels like a grand country estate. Its location, not far off the Silverado Trail (13J—17N) and across the narrow northern end of Napa Valley from the town of St. Helena, is one of Napa's best. Founding and managing partner H. William ("Bill") Harlan is also the proprietor of one of Napa's most sought-after wines, Harlan Estate, and he has pulled out all the stops to make Meadowood a haven for Napa vintners. The annual Napa Valley Wine Auction is held at Meadowood, the vintners' association meets there, and many winery owners are members. The on-site wine education program is excellent, the musical entertainment calendar includes popular local events (such as al fresco opera), and the dining is outstanding even by Napa's high standards.

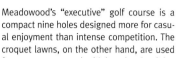

Meadowood's "executive" golf course is a compact nine holes designed more for casual enjoyment than intense competition. The croquet lawns, on the other hand, are used for tournaments at the highest levels of the game. Jerry Stark, Meadowood's teaching pro, works skillfully with players at all levels, including complete novices. If you plan to play, bring white attire. The pro shop, tennis courts, pools, and spa are all well equipped and well run, and the staff (including teaching pros) who administer them are exemplary: professional and responsive when you need them, invisible when you don't. From $345.

CONTACT: **Meadowood Resort,** 900 Meadowood La., St. Helena 94574, tel. 707/895—2461 or 800/458—8080, www.meadowood.com. Member, Relais & Chateaux.

OPTIONS: It would be easy to spend days at Meadowood without ever getting in your car. Still, you're in the Napa Valley and should visit the outside world once in a while. Napa's vineyards and wineries radiate in three directions just minutes from Meadowood's front gate, and your personal guest service manager can help you plot a strategy for visiting the places that interest you most. Meadowood also makes a convenient base for exploring "art without the museum." When you're not dining in the Meadowood grill or restaurant, St. Helena offers excellent options nearby. Established standouts include **Pinot Blanc** (tel. 707/963—6191), **Terra** (tel. 707/963—8931), and **Tra Vigne** (tel. 707/963—4444). Two of Napa's best-known restaurateurs recently opened new places in St. Helena: Cindy Pawlcyn the **Miramonte Restaurant and Café** (tel. 707/963—1200) and Pat Kuleto the **Martini House** (tel. 707/963—2233). St. Helena is also home to numerous galleries and shops, and the **Napa Valley Wine Library** (1492 Library La., tel. 707/963—5244) offers wine buffs thousands of books, tapes, and other materials on wine and Napa's vinous history. If you want to play a more challenging golf course in Napa Valley itself, choices are limited. The **Vintner's Golf Club** in Yountville is only nine holes, but with three sets of tees (7901 Solano Ave., Yountville, tel. 707/944—1992). Farther down the valley in the city of Napa is the 18-hole **Napa Golf Course at Kennedy Park** (Streblow Dr., tel. 707/255—4333). If you've got friends in Napa or

reciprocal rights at your country club back home, try to wangle an invitation to play at **Silverado Country Club,** long the home course of golf great Johnnie Miller.

NAPA VALLEY MUSTARD FESTIVAL (16N–17P)
Napa's Secret Season, p. 28

Years ago, the beauty of Napa in mustard season began attracting photographers, who ultimately formed a friendly contest to showcase their most evocative photos. The contest become a festival, which begins in February with an opening gala, **Mustard Magic.** Barrel tastings and auctions, a gourmet feast, and music and dance fill the halls at this memorable event. In the weeks that follow, wineries and restaurants host special events designed to lift winter spirits to summer highs. All over the valley, chefs and visual artists compete to honor the local mustard in ever more creative ways. The photo finish brings it all to an exhilarating close with wine, music, and dancing late into the night. Between the highlights of the festival, its original inspiration is all around you. At any hour of the day you can walk outside or pull off the road to enjoy the best event of all: golden mustard glowing between endless rows of silent, sleeping vines.

CONTACT: Summers-McCann Public Relations, Sonoma, tel. 707/938—1133, ext. 106, www.mustardfestival.com. This agency has details on all events, including guidelines for entering the Photo Finish and visual-art competitions, attending winery dinners, and participating in sporting events.

LODGING: A top location for Mustard Festival visitors is **Auberge du Soleil,** which overlooks Napa's mustard-gold vinelands and is well situated to catch maximum rays from the late-winter sun. It's also just up the hill from the Silverado Trail, the best route for viewing the mustard while cruising between events and wineries. 180 Rutherford Hill Rd., Rutherford 94573, tel. 707/963—1211, www.aubergedusoleil.com. Cottages range from cozy to expansive. Spa, boutique, restaurant, and one of Napa's best bars. From $450 during the festival. Convenient lodging, especially for families attending the festival's Market Fair, is available at **Embassy Suites Napa Valley,** which offers two pools, a wildlife garden, abundant parking, and other amenities not far from Napa's burgeoning downtown restaurant scene. If you're with children, get a room downstairs. Otherwise request an upper floor. 1075 California Blvd., Napa 94559, tel. 707/253—9540 or 800/EMBASSY, www.embassynapa.com. 205 suites, from $174 during the festival.

OPTIONS: Because the tourist crush is still months away, Napa in February and March can be heaven for wine explorers. Restaurant reservations are easy to come by, local vintners are out in force at their favorite eateries, and wine tasting rooms are blissfully uncrowded. One caveat: many wineries are bottling previous vintages at this time of year, so if you're determined to meet winemakers, make an appointment. If you're making a day trip, get picnic goodies or a quick lunch at **Oakville Grocery** in Oakville (tel. 707/944—8802) or **Gordon's Cafe and Wine Bar** (tel. 707/944—8246) in Yountville. Dining in downtown Napa instead of "up-valley" shortens your evening drive back to the San Francisco Bay area to well under an hour. **Celadon** (tel. 707/254—9690), **Chanterelle** (tel. 707/253—7300), **Cole's Chop House** (tel. 707/224—6328), **Misto** (tel. 707/252—4080), **Pearl** (tel. 707/224—9161), and **Tuscany** (tel. 707/258—1000) are all worth a meal in any season, and all are likely to be celebrating the Mustard Festival in some way.

NAPA'S GLAMOROUS NIEBAUM-COPPOLA ESTATE (15L)
Return to Glory, p. 48

The historic Inglenook Winery was completed in 1888 by owner Gustav Niebaum and his ranch manager, Hamden W. McIntyre, who doubled as winery designer. They created the building to project an image of stature and strength equivalent to the famed Bordeaux châteaus that Niebaum knew from his travels, and it still presents that imposing countenance. After Niebaum's heirs lost control of Inglenook and lackluster corporate ownership had drained the property of its appeal, fate intervened. Good timing and a few hits, including *Bram Stoker's Dracula*, enabled Francis Ford Coppola to purchase the winery and recombine it with the estate's original vineyard and woodland acreage. Coppola affects a modest, son-of-immigrants persona for the media, but he's a consummate showman, and in Niebaum he found a spiritual forefather. While the earlier man made his big statement with architecture, Coppola makes his with a filmlike winery visit, complete with storylined visual displays, movie props, and a tasting suite that's almost dizzyingly over the top.

CONTACT: Niebaum-Coppola Estate Winery, 1991 St. Helena Hwy., Rutherford 94573, tel. 707/968—1100. Public tours are given at 10:30 am and 2:30 pm daily, on a first-come-first-served basis. An extra tour is added on Saturdays, at 12:30 pm. For private tours call the main number; for concierge services call 707/968—1177. While wine-tasting you can also purchase wine accoutrements, books, clothing, and Coppola's films on video and DVDs.

DISTANCES: Rutherford is the northernmost of Napa Valley's three mid-valley towns (the others are Yountville and Oakville) along Highway 29, known locally as St. Helena Highway. 60 mi from San Francisco.

LODGING: Rutherford's best and most historic lodging is **Rancho Caymus Inn,** with 26 suites, each named for a colorful (and sometimes notorious) individual out of Napa's past. The inn is owned by the Komes family, which also owns Flora Springs Winery. 140 Rutherford Rd., Rutherford 94573, tel. 800/845—1777. All suites include phone, TV, honor bar, A/C, coffeemaker, refrigerator, and breakfast. Upstairs suites include courtyard balconies, and the four largest suites offer built-in whirlpool tubs. The courtyard and fountain of the Spanish Colonial main building offer a cool respite from wine-tasting rounds. From $195.

OPTIONS: When it was built, utilizing mammoth stones quarried on the site and reinforced with iron bars, Inglenook Winery (now Niebaum-Coppola) amazed visitors and gave a rustic farm valley called Napa an early taste of romance and glamour. The winery's design was quickly emulated by other wealthy men in Napa Valley, and you can see good examples at **Trefethen Winery** (1160 Oak Knoll Ave. Napa, tel. 707/255—7700) and the former Greystone Winery, now the **Culinary Institute of America** (2555 St. Helena Hwy., St. Helena, tel. 707/963—4503). Rutherford and nearby Oakville are home to numerous landmark wineries, all on or near Highway 29, including **Beaulieu Vineyards** (tel. 707/963—2411), **Cakebread Winery**

(tel. 707/963–5221), **Grgich Hills Cellars** (tel. 707/963–2784), **Opus One** (tel. 707/944–9442), and **Robert Mondavi Winery** (tel. 707/963–9311). For a quick lunch or picnic supplies, visit **Oakville Grocery** (7856 St. Helena Hwy., tel. 707/944–8802) or **Pometta's Deli** (7787 St. Helena Hwy., tel. 707/944–2365). For dinner, Rancho Caymus Inn is home to one of Napa's newest nationally recognized restaurants, **La Toque**—fancy French cuisine with California accents.

CARLO MARCHIORI'S VILLA IN CALISTOGA, NAPA VALLEY (12J)
Master of Illusion, p. 44

A Venetian Carnival and *commedia dell'arte*. Pompeian frescoes and the Roman Forum. Theatrical fountains and sensuous sculptures. To experience all these facets of Italian history and culture would take weeks, but you can immerse yourself in all of them at once with a visit to Villa Ca'Toga, home and workshop of world-renowned master artist Carlo Marchiori. Marchiori's work graces public buildings and private residences around the world, perhaps most notably the famed Raffles Hotel in Singapore, where he has created dozens of witty, sharp-eyed tableaus. Marchiori started building on the site with a corrugated tin barn. Over time he has transformed it inside and out into a true Italian villa: a place where house and grounds create an idealized world within the world. Watch out for the sharp wit, though. One seemingly ancient Latin phrase carved in a fallen lintel reads: "Non tecum non sine te vivere possum." The translation? "I can't live with you or without you."

CONTACT: Ca'Toga Galleria d'Arte, 1206 Cedar St., Calistoga 94515, tel. 707/942–3900, fax 707/942–3939, www.catoga.com. Guided tours are given Saturday mornings May–October, and you must have a reservation.

DISTANCES: 27 mi from downtown Napa, 75 mi from San Francisco. Driving instructions will be given when you reserve your tour.

LODGING: Ca'Toga stands on the northern fringe of Calistoga, the Napa Valley's historic spa town (*see* "Steam Heat"), so any Calistoga lodging puts you minutes away. In downtown Calistoga, within walking distance of many spas, restaurants, and other attractions, is the venerable **Mount View Hotel,** 1457 Lincoln Ave., Calistoga 94515, tel. 707/942–6877 or 800/816–6877, fax 707/942–6904. Amenities include an on-site spa, heated pool, evening entertainment, and Catahoula, one of Calistoga's finer restaurants. Three cottages with private patios, hot tubs, and wet bars, 8 suites with period furniture, 22 rooms with TV, phone, and feather beds. From $165.

OPTIONS: After your visit to Ca'Toga, plan to visit Marchiori's gallery, **Ca'Toga Galleria d'Arte** (1206 Cedar St., tel. 707/942–3900, fax 707/942–3939, www.catoga.com), in downtown Calistoga. There you'll find everything from 50¢ postcard reproductions to $5,000 original works. Even if you're not shopping, you'll be gawking at the ceiling, where Marchiori depicts the starry heavens teeming with zodiacal and mythical beings (look closely and you'll find his own visage among them). Just steps away is the **Sharpsteen Museum,** a compact, engaging collection lovingly supported by Calistogans, including Marchiori himself. If you want to get off your feet and relax, it's only a few short blocks to the **Lavender Hill Spa,** one of the first places in Calistoga to forego segregated treatment facilities and the standard mud bath in favor of a European-style, couples experience that some say is even more invigorating (Hwy. 29 at Lincoln Ave., tel. 707/942–4495). You'll need a reservation at most spas to ensure that you get the treatment you want, especially in summer and on holiday weekends, so plan accordingly. **Château Montelena,** one of Napa's landmark wineries, is close to Ca'Toga and worth a visit for its wine and its grounds (1429 Tubbs La., tel. 707/942–5105). The winery's picnic areas, including a small lake with islands, are so popular that people reserve a spot months in advance. Put your own picnic together at **Palisades Market** (1506 Lincoln Ave., between Fairway and Brannan, tel. 707/942–9549). For lunch or dinner, don't miss **Wappo** (1226B Washington St., above Lincoln Ave., tel. 707/942–4712), which has some of the most eclectic delicious food in the wine country and a cozy, vine-draped courtyard in which to enjoy it.

TOP TABLES IN YOUNTVILLE, NAPA VALLEY

(15–16M)

Bring Your Appetite, p. 68

Yountville is known to many people as the home of The French Laundry, the invention of chef Thomas Keller, the darling of national critics. Getting a reservation requires months of determined phoning or an unforeseeable stroke of good fortune, and the cost of one meal there feeds you for days anywhere else. So don't make it the centerpiece of an escape to the Napa Valley. Instead, explore the bounty and variety of Yountville's other outstanding cafés and restaurants. You'll see how Napa's wine industry drinks and dines (very well indeed), and you'll have more memories to take home. Reservations at traditional mealtimes are always a good idea. If the weather is fine you may want to dine al fresco—most restaurants listed below have outdoor seating—so bring a sweater just in case. Casual attire is appropriate during the day, but at night you'll feel more comfortable if you dress up a bit.

CONTACTS: Bistro Jeanty, 6510 Washington St., tel. 707/944–0103. Daily 11:30–11. French comfort food prepared with panache. **Bouchon,** 6534 Washington St., tel. 707/944–8037. Lunch daily 11:30–2:30, dinner Sun.–Thurs. 5:30–12:30, Fri. and Sat. 5:30–1. Full bar, French country classics. **Brix,** 7737 St. Helena Hwy. (Hwy. 29), tel. 707/944–2749. Lunch daily 11:30–4, dinner daily 5–11 (seating until 9:30). Full bar, creative "New Century" cuisine. **Domaine Chandon,** 1 California Dr., tel. 707/944–1123 or 800/934–3975. Lunch daily 11:30–2:30 except Mon. and Tues. Nov.–Mar., dinner daily 6–11, except Mon. and Tues. in Dec. and Jan. Refined California cuisine. **Gordon's Café and Wine Bar,** 6770 Washington St., tel. 707/944–8246. Breakfast and lunch daily 8–6, dinner (reservation essential) Fri. at 7. The best place to start your day. **Piatti,** 6480 Washington St., tel. 707/944–2070. Daily 11–11. Full bar; the Italian original that launched the successful chain. **The French Laundry,** 6640 Washington St., tel. 707/944–2380. Lunch Fri.–Sun. 11–1, dinner (reservations essential) daily 5:30–9:30. Ultra-refined French-American cuisine.

DISTANCES: 55 mi from San Francisco, 9 mi from downtown Napa, 12 mi from St. Helena.

LODGING: If you're going to eat your way through Yountville, you'll need to work off a few calories. **Villagio** is Yountville's only spa hotel, and it's within walking distance of every restaurant in the above list except for Brix (which is approximately three minutes away by car). Villagio Inn & Spa, 6481 Washington St., Yountville 94599, tel. 800/351–1133, fax 707/944–8855, www.villagio.com. In addition to a workout room, lap pool, and tennis courts, the 3,500-square-foot spa has an attentive staff ready to massage out the kinks; rub and wrap you with mud, herbs, and grape seed; or give you a facial. Your pores will positively tingle after you treat yourself to a hydrotherapy tub with underwater massage, a sauna, and a Vichy shower. Two outdoor heated pools, two tennis courts, and a golf course nearby. The 112 rooms all have wood-burning fireplaces, refrigerators, AC, TV, telephone, hair dryers, fluffy bathrobes, and a welcoming bottle of wine. Continental Champagne breakfast in the morning and complimentary coffee, tea, and cookies in the afternoon are included. From $225. Just down the street is Villagio's companion property, **Vintage Inn.** It's a bit older, which you may prefer for the lusher foliage, more spacious layout, and patio off your ground-floor room. All amenities and spa privileges are the same as at Villagio. 80 rooms, from $200. Reserve through Villagio.

OPTIONS: Yountville is the nearest town to the **Stags Leap District** (16M), Napa's most compact "appellation" (officially designated winegrowing area), which is one of the very top areas for growing Napa Valley Cabernet Sauvignon. Furthermore, the wineries are smaller and more intimate than the big, touristy wineries to the north. That makes Stags Leap a great destination for a wine-tasting weekend, because you can visit multiple wineries and compare numerous wines without too much driving. **Stag's Leap Wine Cellars** (tel. 707/944–2020), **Shafer Vineyards** (tel. 707/944–2877), **Robert Sinskey Vineyards** (tel. 707/944–9090), and **Silverado Vineyards** (tel. 707/257–1770) are among the better-known wineries in the district, but a dozen others also make wine worth tasting and welcome visitors. (www.stagsleapdistrict.com.) **Domaine Chandon** (1 California Dr., tel. 707/944–1123 or 800/934–3975) is one of California's oldest and largest producers of sparkling wines, where you can learn the differences between wine with bubbles and wine without. It is open later than most wineries. **Vintage 1870** (6525 Washington St., tel. 707/944—2451), near Bistro Jeanty and Bouchon, is a complex of 36 shops and galleries that can easily swallow an entire afternoon. In late fall, when Yountville lights up its downtown for the holiday season, there's an annual **Festival of Lights** that's fun for families. Call 707/944—0904 or visit www.yountville.com.

SONOMA

Sonoma County is the cradle of northern California's wine country. While vineyards were planted earlier in other places, commercial winemaking flowered faster and more fully in Sonoma Valley than in the neighboring Napa Valley. Sonoma Valley is, in some ways, a smaller version of its cousin to the east: a crescent shape that arches from San Francisco Bay in the south to Santa Rosa (10L–11N) in the north. It's much narrower, though, and more rural, which for many people makes it more charming. North of Santa Rosa is Alexander Valley, a winegrowing region that shares its major hub, Healdsburg (9J), with the Russian River Valley (6M–7L) to the west. These two Sonoma wine valleys are strikingly different. Alexander Valley is a flat, fertile flood plain along the Russian River, and many of its grapes are sold to wineries in other regions. Russian River Valley is a hilly, heavily forested area dotted with small vineyards and winery estates that proudly put their own names on their labels. To the north and west is yet another premium Sonoma winegrowing area, Dry Creek Valley (7I–8J), where 100-year-old Italian family wineries are still nestled in among glamorous newcomers.

SONOMA'S SPECTACULAR WINE ESTATE GARDEN
Estate of Serenity, p. 16

The 5 acres of gardens that surround Villa Fiore are worth a visit even if you never set foot in the tasting room—though you shouldn't miss that experience either. The "bones" of the garden are its trees: more than 30 species, including numerous exotic imports and dwarf varieties. Many of the individual beds complement a centerpiece set of trees with flowering shrubs and grasses, in turn bordered by annuals. Highlights are the tulips and irises that appear late March or early April. When bulb season passes, another palette of floral color is quickly laid on, and this process continues through the fall. In California, roses bloom for much of the year, so Rhonda Carano's arbor of personally selected rose varieties is usually in good form. The personal touch rules here—Ferrari-Carano's gardeners work diligently by hand, even when trimming hedges. The tasting room is a model of the genre, with the inevitable commercial aspects kept in balance with the surrounding beauty.

CONTACT: Ferrari-Carano Vineyards and Winery, 8761 Dry Creek Rd., Healdsburg 95448, tel. 707/433—6700, fax 707/431—1742, www.ferrari-carano.com

DISTANCES: 70 mi from San Francisco. Take U.S. 101 north, exit at Dry Creek Road, and proceed west approximately 8 mi. The winery will be on your left past the intersection of Dutcher Creek Road. Approximately 10 mi from downtown Healdsburg; take Healdsburg Boulevard north from the plaza and turn left on Dry Creek Road.

LODGING: If you like what Rhonda and Don Carano are doing with Villa Fiore, you may want to experience their hospitality at **Vintners Inn,** which they purchased in 2000 and are turning into a luxury wine-country resort hotel. Set in a 90-acre vineyard on the northern edge of Santa Rosa, Sonoma County's largest city, the property has 44 high-ceiling, Mediterranean-style rooms with private balconies or patios and fireplaces. Outdoor whirlpool, in-room spa services, and concierge offerings head a growing list of resort-type touches. 4350 Barnes Rd., Santa Rosa, tel. 800/421—2584, www.vintnersinn.com. From $193. Closer to Ferrari-Carano, in the town of Healdsburg, is longtime standout **Madrona Manor,** with nine rooms in a grand, gabled 1881 Victorian mansion and another eight rooms and seven suites in a former carriage house and other outbuildings. 1001 Westside Rd., Healdsburg, tel. 707/433—4231, www.madronamanor.com. All rooms with full private bath, in-room phone, and full breakfast; 18 accommodations also have fireplaces and eight have a balcony or deck. A pool and 8 acres of gardens complete the setting. From $210.

OPTIONS: Dry Creek Valley is home to wineries of all styles and personalities, so a weekend of winery touring there rarely becomes repetitive as it sometimes does in better-known areas. Lou Preston of **Preston Vineyards** (9282 Dry Creek Rd., tel. 707/433—3372) is notable for recently getting out of the mega-production rat race and going back to Sonoma's roots: small lots of individualistic, estate-made wines. Those roots were set down by people like Italian immigrant Amerigo Rafanelli, whose **A. Rafanelli Winery** (4685 Dry Creek Rd., tel. 707/433—1385) still produces exceptional Zinfandel under the family name. **Pedroncelli Winery** (1220 Canyon Rd., Geyserville, tel. 707/857—3531) and **Pezzi-King Vineyards** (3805 Lambert Bridge Rd., Healdsburg, tel. 707/431—9388 or 800/411—4758) are two other favorites with visitors to the area for their relaxed, friendly welcome and exemplary Cabernet Sauvignons and Zinfandels. Both Vintners Inn and Madrona Manor, described above, offer excellent restaurants, though both are outside the valley. During a wine-tasting weekend you can simply stop in for basic picnic makings at **Dry Creek Store** near the intersection of Dry Creek and Lambert Bridge roads (3495 Dry Creek Rd., Healdsburg, tel. 707/433—4171), and eat al fresco at a winery. If you desire something more substantial or sophisticated, the **Oakville Grocery** in downtown Healdsburg (124 Matheson St., tel. 707/433—3200) is a good place to start. While on the plaza, you can also shop at Rhonda Carano's **Seasons of the Vineyard** (113 Plaza St., tel. 707/431—2222, fax 707/431—2208), an arts and antiques shop packed with imported and local finds for home, garden, and gifts.

RIDING JACK LONDON'S RANCH IN SONOMA (13N)
Western Frontier, p. 38

Jack London State Historical Park spans 800 acres of the 1,400-acre Beauty Ranch that London assembled between 1905 and 1911, on scenic uplands between the village of Glen Ellen (13N) and rugged Mt. Sonoma (12N). In 1959, the state of California began acquiring portions of Beauty Ranch, including the ruins of London's tragic mansion called Wolf House, his widow Charmian's House of Happy Walls (now a museum), and Lon-

don's final resting place. Before or after you visit these attractions on foot, the best way to see the land is on a ride with the Sonoma Cattle Company. Rides in the park operate from April to November, weather permitting. Reservations are required. In August and September, the vineyards are verdant and the grapes hang in fat bunches. After the harvest, the vineyards glow auburn and gold—a beautiful sight on a fall afternoon.

CONTACT: Sonoma Cattle Company, Box 877, Glen Ellen 95442, tel. and fax 707/996—8566, www.winecountrytrailrides.com. Jack London State Historical Park, 2400 London Ranch Rd., Glen Ellen 95442, tel. 707/938—5216.

DISTANCES: 7 mi from downtown Sonoma via Highway 12 (also known as the Sonoma Highway). 15 mi from Santa Rosa via Highway 12, 65 mi from San Francisco via Santa Rosa, 45 mi from San Francisco via Sonoma.

LODGING: Two of Sonoma's finer hostelries are near the park. **Gaige House Inn** is a service-oriented B&B housed in an 1890 Queen Anne mansion in the quiet village of Glen Ellen. Features include impressive orchids and lovely gardens along a creek and, rare for a B&B, a swimming pool. Breakfast is exceptional. 13540 Arnold Dr., Glen Ellen, tel. 707/935—0237 or 800/935—0237. 6 rooms from $150, 5 suites from $325. **Kenwood Inn & Spa** is a captivating island of Italian villa-style comforts plus a pool, hot tub, and full spa facility bordered by vineyards on one side and an oak grove on another. 10400 Sonoma Hwy., Kenwood, tel. 707/833—1293. 12 rooms with fireplaces and full breakfast, from $255.

OPTIONS: If horses aren't an attractive mode of conveyance, you can also hike in Jack London State Historic Park on many of the same trails used by **Sonoma Cattle Company** (13N), the sole concessionaire for horseback rides. The same outfit also takes horses and riders into Sugarloaf Ridge State Park (13L—14M) in nearby Kenwood (13M). Rides there operate year-round, so you can take in wildflowers in February and March. Overnight rides with campground stays are also available, giving you a chance to take in views of the San Francisco Bay area at sunset. Near Jack London State Historical Park, the town of Glen Ellen offers a surprising number of interesting shops and places to eat. **Glen Ellen Village Market** (13751 Arnold Dr., tel. 707/996—

6728) is a good place for picnic supplies and drinks to beat the heat. **Garden Court Café and Bakery,** outside the park entrance (13875 Sonoma Hwy., Glen Ellen, tel. 707/935—3386), draws crowds for its substantial burgers and sandwiches. **Jack London Bookstore** (14300 Arnold Dr., tel. 707/996—2888) specializes in the author's books and other regional literature. Sondra Bernstein has moved her much-loved The Girl & the Fig restaurant to downtown Sonoma, but she's given Glen Ellen **The Girl & the Gaucho** (13690 Arnold Dr., tel. 707/938—2130), which serves eclectic food derived from Latin America. Dinner only; reservations recommended. Nearby wineries include Arrowood, B.R. Cohn, Glen Ellen, and Kenwood.

WHIMSICAL JIMTOWN (91)

Oddball Artifacts In The Alexander Valley, Sonoma, p 32.

Carrie Brown and John Werner discovered Jimtown on the Fourth of July in 1987, while visiting the wine country from New York. They were looking at a run-down former post office that had been abandoned for years. What they created was a quintessential country store, the kind that caters to everyone because it's the only one around. The shelves in the front of the store are jammed with an eclectic array of the oddball and childlike alongside the elegant and practical, so browse carefully or you may miss something you didn't know you wanted. Carrie's parents, Caroline and Charlie, operate the "Mercantile and Exchange" part of the business, and you may see them arranging artifacts or explaining the workings of an antique fly reel. The food, to take out or eat on the premises, is fresh and zesty, and the coffee has bite. Breakfast and lunch are served all day. Some sandwiches may feature Jimtown's own condiments (such as the chopped olive or spicy chipotle spreads), which are also for sale.

CONTACT: Jimtown Store, 6706 Hwy. 128, Healdsburg 95448, tel. 707/433—1212, fax 707/433—1252, www.jimtown.com. Weekdays 7—5, weekends 7:30—5.

DISTANCES: 70 mi from San Francisco. Take U.S. 101 North to Hwy. 128 East (from Geyserville) or the Alexander Valley Road exit.

LODGING: Bed-and-breakfasts don't get more Victorian than the **Hope-Merrill House,** an 1880s mansion that served as the stage-coach stop in the days when wealthy San Franciscans rode up to take the thermal waters in the geysers above Alexander Valley. 21253 Geyserville Ave., Box 42, Geyserville 95441, tel. 800/825—4233, www.hope-inns.com. Those who adore Victorian ruffles and bric-a-brac will be in heaven. Those who don't can instead admire the extraordinary woodwork and wainscoting, the pressed-metal ceilings, and the hands-on winemaking program for guests each fall. Everyone will enjoy the pool, shaded by persimmon and fig trees. 7 rooms and 1 suite, all with queen beds and private baths. Fireplaces and/or whirlpool baths in some rooms. The suite has a TV. From $215. To imagine your life as an Alexander Valley vintner, call Carol at **Robert Young Estate Winery** (tel. 707/433—1259) and ask if the guest house is available. Breakfast is not included, but the Wolf range, hot tub, and flagstone terrace will make you feel enough at home to prepare your own—or you can simply roll down the hill to the Jimtown Store.

OPTIONS: Highway 128, which runs through the heart of Alexander Valley for most of its length, is a joy to drive (except, perhaps, at the height of harvest, when tractors roll along at 5 mph). Much of the time the road is elevated just enough to give you expansive vineyard views without separating you from the scenery. The highway exits the valley toward Napa on the southern end. On the northern end, it continues up to Mendocino, the Anderson Valley, and the Pacific Ocean. There are wineries along the way, and many of them are still friendly family-owned places where visitors are genuinely welcome. Alexander Valley wineries with established national reputations include **Alexander Valley Vineyards** (tel. 707/433—7209 or 800/888—7209), **Château Souverain** (tel. 707/433—8281 or 888/809—4637), **Geyser Peak Winery** (tel. 800/255—9463), **Murphy-Goode Estate Winery** (tel. 707/431—7644 or 800/499—7644), **Seghesio Family Vineyards** (tel. 707/433—7102), and **Simi Winery** (tel. 707/433—6981 or 800/746—4880). **Healdsburg** is where you will find nearly all the region's cultural life, including inns, restaurants, shops, and galleries. Yet it's possible to find gems just as bright without confining yourself to town. **Château Souverain** (tel. 707/433–3141) is one of the few wineries in California allowed to operate a restaurant, and it has a good one (with a terrace for outdoor dining). The tiny town of Geyserville now boasts a fine Italian restaurant, **Santi** (tel. 707/857–1790), and a Western-style barbecue saloon, **Geyser Smokehouse** (tel. 707/857–4600). **Bosworth & Son General Merchandise** in Geyserville (just down the street from Hope-Merrill House) is worth a visit if you need a hat, Western wear, or some tack for your horse.

BARREL TASTING ON THE RUSSIAN RIVER WINE ROAD, SONOMA (7L–9I)
Back Roads & Barrel Samples, p. 22

Just a few months after harvest, wineries in Sonoma County's Russian River Valley open their doors—and tap their barrels—for intrepid visitors from across the country. The friendly, informal, free weekend event falls in early March, when temperatures might be in the balmy 70s or the rain-lashed 40s. Vineyards and wineries are small in the Russian River Valley, a legacy of the area's immigrant history and complex topography, so the scenery is as intimate as the scene inside the wineries. Presiding vintners sip hot coffee while you sip Pinot Noir, Chardonnay, and other wines drawn directly from American and French oak barrels. Many Russian River wineries can presell everything they make, but hold back a portion to sell at their own winery—beginning on the barrel tasting weekend. If you covet those wines, arrive early at your chosen wineries and then let the rest of your weekend unwind on the back roads and in the small towns that dot the region.

CONTACT: Russian River Wine Rd., Box 46, Healdsburg 95448, tel. 800/723–6336, www.wineroad.com.

DISTANCES: There are numerous routes into the Russian River Valley. From San Francisco, the simplest is to take U.S. 101 north to Cotati (11N–O) and then Highway 116 west to the wine country. Russian River Wine Road has maps on-line (and prints more portable versions) that show the other possibilities. If you stay overnight in the region, your innkeepers will be an excellent source of information as well.

LODGING: If you can plan well ahead, book a room at the

Applewood Inn and Restaurant. The location is convenient to major wine routes, and the accommodations gracefully blend rustic redwood and stone exteriors with gardens, terraces, balconies, and rooms with antique furnishings. The restaurant is one of the best around. 13555 Hwy. 116, Guerneville 95446, tel. 707/869–9093, fax 707/869–9170, www.applewoodinn.com. 19 rooms, some with fireplaces, Jacuzzis, or verandas; outdoor pool, hot tub, and full breakfast. From $155. A little deeper into the woods is the **Inn at Occidental** (8M), a restored Victorian mansion nestled among tall trees and replete with antiques and heirlooms. 3657 Church St., Occidental 95465, tel. 707/874–1047 or 800/522–6324, fax 707/874–1078, www.innatoccidental.com. 16 rooms with private baths and fireplaces; some rooms also have spa tubs or hot tubs. Full breakfast, afternoon tea, evening wine and hors d'oeuvres. From $195. For a more intimate B&B experience, consider **Vine Hill Inn Bed & Breakfast**. 3949 Vine Hill Rd., Sebastopol 95472, tel. 707/823–8832, fax 707/824–1045. 4 bedrooms with private baths; pool, porches, decks with vineyard and mountain views. From $135.

OPTIONS: You can comfortably visit up to half a dozen wineries in a day that even includes a leisurely lunch. The better-known wineries, such as **Davis Bynum Winery** (9K) (tel. 800/826–1073) **Iron Horse** (tel. 707/887–1507), **La Crema** (tel. 800/769–3649), **Rochioli** (tel. 707/433–2305), and **Joseph Swan** (tel. 707/573–3747), get crowded in the afternoon so plan to visit them in the morning, if possible. For lunch, make a midday stop at **Russian River Vineyards** in Forestville (8–9L), where in addition to barrel tasting you'll find **Topolos** (tel. 707/887–1562), a rustic garden restaurant serving savory Greek and Mediterranean cuisine. Options for evening dining continue to expand. **The Farmhouse Inn** in Forestville (tel. 707/887–3300) has added a gourmet wine-country restaurant, and nearby Healdsburg is full of excellent restaurants, including **Bistro Ralph** (tel. 707/433–1380), **Madrona Manor** (tel. 707/433–4231), **Charcuterie** (tel. 707/431–7213), and **Zin** (707/473–0946). If you prefer to drink and not drive, consider booking a driver for the day or weekend. Local innkeepers recommend **Beau Limousine,** and can make arrangements for you or recommend alternatives. A growing number of wineries open their barrel rooms on the Friday before the weekend. Find out which ones by joining the **RoadRunners** club of the Russian River Wine Road. The annual membership fee of $25 single/$40 couple includes advance information about the barrel–tasting weekend, periodic newsletters, and invitations to exclusive events throughout the year. www.wineroad.com/club.

THE 19TH-CENTURY MISSION TOWN OF SONOMA (14–O)
Wine Country Epicenter, p. 66

None of northern California's wine towns is so drenched in history as Sonoma—and none has as many important wineries so close to the town center. Spanish missionaries capped their conquests, Mexico reached its northern apex, the United States ended the Bear Flag Revolt, and General Mariano Vallejo launched the region's first commercial winery—all in Sonoma. You can discern the layers of history by standing in the plaza and looking at the buildings that surround it. Most of the ground-floor adobes date from the mid-1800s. Second stories were added near the turn of the century, when the wine business was getting established. Buildings with a third floor, such as the Sonoma Hotel, got them even later. Count Agoston Haraszthy, firmly ensconced in the history books as the father of California wine, brought 300 different grape varieties from Europe in 1857 and cultivated them 2 mi from the plaza at his Buena Vista Winery. The Gundlach-Bundschu, Ravenswood, and Sebastiani wineries are also just a short distance from the center, knitting the wine industry into city life in a way that is rare in California.

CONTACT: Sonoma State Historic Park, W. Spain St. at 3rd St., tel. 707/938–1519. One ticket is good for all park sites in and around the central plaza, including **Mission San Francisco Solano de Sonoma,** the **Sonoma Barracks,** the **Toscano Hotel,** Vallejo's former home and gardens at **Lachryma Montis,** and others.

DISTANCES: Sonoma is 33 mi from San Francisco.

LODGING: The **El Dorado Hotel** puts you right on the plaza, in an historic building to boot. 405 1st St. W, Sonoma 95476, tel. 800/289–3031 or 707/996–3030, fax 707/996–3148,

www.hoteleldorado.com. The 26 comfortable rooms all have balconies overlooking either the plaza or the courtyard with its impressive fig tree. Private baths and TV are included in all rooms, along with a welcoming bottle of wine and Continental breakfast (which you can take into the courtyard). A heated lap pool is available, if you don't get enough exercise walking or biking around town. From $165. For B&B fanciers, **Victorian Garden Inn** is just steps off the plaza behind a lush, beautifully tended garden. 316 E. Napa St., Sonoma 95476, tel. 800543–5339 or 707/996–5339, fax 707/996–1689, www.victoriangardeninn.com. The 1870s farmhouse and water tower contain four compact guest rooms with period furnishings. The three water-tower rooms have private baths; the room in the main house has an adjacent bath. The wraparound porch, swimming pool, and garden will keep you from spending much time indoors. From $119.

OPTIONS: The wineries in the town of Sonoma have engaging personalities and interesting histories attached to them, making them all worth a visit. Best of all, you can get to them on foot or by bicycle. **Buena Vista Carneros Estate** (18000 Old Winery Rd., tel. 707/252–7117) is the current name of Haraszthy's original 19th-century winery, and the shady courtyard is a good picnic spot. The Sebastiani family has been central to Sonoma for three generations, and the recent restoration of the **Sebastiani Vineyards** winery two blocks from the plaza (389 4th St. E, tel. 707/933–3200) demonstrates continued commitment. They also have a tasting room at the southwest corner of the plaza, called Sebastiani on the Square (103 W. Napa St., tel. 707/933–3291. **Ravenswood** (18701 Gehricke Rd., tel. 707/938–1960) is the home base of master winemaker Joel Peterson, whose Zinfandel is a benchmark for that most Sonoman of red wines. Another historic, often overlooked Sonoma winery, **Gundlach-Bundschu** (2000 Denmark St., tel. 707/938–5277), is worth a visit for its rapidly improving wines and the hilltop adjacent to the winery, from which you can survey the city and valley. To rent a bicycle, ask at your inn or hotel, or call **Goodtime Touring Company** (tel. 707/938–0453, www.goodtimetouring.com), which organizes excursions and rentals, and even picks up the wine you buy—while you're out biking—and ships it home for you. The plaza is ringed with restaurants of all sizes and descriptions, so as you walk around during the day keep an eye out for dining rooms and menus that might appeal to you in the evening. Sonoma vintners frequent **The Girl and the Fig** (tel. 707/938—3634), and everybody goes to **Piatti** (tel. 707/996—2351) in the El Dorado Hotel; both offer outdoor seating. **Maya** (tel. 707/935—3500) is a welcome addition to the plaza dining scene, with authentic southeastern Mexican dishes. A few blocks from the square, **The General's Daughter** (400 W. Spain St., tel. 707/938—4004) is housed in an 1864 mansion built for General Mariano Vallejo's daughter Natalie. Pick up picnic goods at **Sonoma Cheese Factory** (tel. 707/996—1931) or **Cucina Viansa** (tel. 707/935—5656). For festivals and events in the town of Sonoma, contact the **Sonoma Valley Visitors Bureau** (53 1st St. E, Sonoma 95476, tel. 707/996—1090, www.sonomavalley.com).

AQUATIC HEALING AT SONOMA MISSION INN
(14–O)
Liquid Bodies, p. 60

At the height of the Jazz Age, Sonoma Mission Inn was created out of the ashes of a hot-springs hotel that burned to the ground in 1923. The thermal springs deep underground were not affected, and today they supply the inn with 135-degree mineral water year-round. The inn's architecture and decor combine the best qualities of the Mission style, introduced to California by Spanish Jesuits in the 1600s and 1700s, with the casual elegance the state is known for today. Public rooms have high ceilings with exposed beams, garden-facing windows, and an abundance of comfortable seating areas. The 10 fully landscaped acres are hidden away from the busy traffic on nearby Sonoma Highway. The inn prides itself on its standing as the wine country's top luxury spa resort, so expect to be pampered—and to pay for the privilege.

CONTACT: Sonoma Mission Inn, 100 Boyes Blvd., Box 1447, Sonoma 95476, tel. 707/938—9000, fax 707/938—4250, www.sonomamissioninn.com.

DISTANCES: 40 mi from San Francisco, 3 mi from downtown Sonoma.

LODGING: The inn has 97 original historic rooms, 71 newer rooms built in 1986, and 60 suites that have been added in the past five years. All come with a complimentary bottle of wine, private bar, TV, room service, twice-daily maid service, well-stocked bathrooms, and the ever-popular fluffy white robe and slippers. Accommodations in the Mission Suite category are ingeniously designed to bring the spa experience into your private chambers; sleeping and bathing spaces are separated not by a wall but by an oversized bathtub or see-through fireplace. Historic rooms from $300, modern rooms from $380, suites from $550.

OPTIONS: The **spa,** completely redone in 2000, operates on the European model, meaning you're expected to get wet as often as possible. Options include the Watsu pools, the swimming pool, private whirlpool and mineral baths, and the Roman bathing ritual, which includes two more thermal pools, half a dozen shower alcoves, and a spacious steam room. **Watsu** is subtle, but unmistakably energizing. The dozens of other personal treatments available include massages, facials, wraps, manicures, and pedicures. The inn also houses a full-service hair salon and a yoga studio where you can take a group class or a private lesson. The **Roman bathing ritual** is included with most treatments, and you should follow your reservationist's advice about arriving in time to take advantage of it. The vineyard-bordered **golf course** is a 7,069-yard, 18-hole, par-72 challenge landscaped with native trees and views of the Mayacamas Mountains (12I–16P) to the east. California-style spa cuisine was pioneered at Sonoma Mission Inn in the 1980s, and **The Restaurant,** under the guidance of executive chef Toni Robertson, has recently renewed its commitment to fabulous food appropriate to a fitness resort. She has also brought more intense flavors to the **Big 3 Diner,** the inn's casual dining option. When it comes time to leave the luxurious confines of the inn, you can find 30 wineries in the surrounding Sonoma Valley, as well as living history in the nearby town of Sonoma (*see* "Wine Country Epicenter") and in Jack London State Historical Park (*see* "Western Frontier").

Thom Elkjer is wine editor for *Wine Country Living* magazine. He has written for *Wine Spectator, Appellation,* and other publications in the U.S. and Europe. His recent nonfiction includes *Adventures in Wine*, a literary exploration of the world's wine country. He is currently plotting a sequel to his award-winning first novel, *Hook, Line and Murder.* He and his wife, the artist Antoinette von Grone, share a home in the California mission town of San Rafael and a farm in the wine country.

British photographer Robert Holmes launched his distinguished career covering the 1975 British Everest Expedition for the London Daily Mail. He has since traveled the world for major magazines, including *National Geographic, Islands, Travel Holiday, Geo, Life,* and T*ravel + Leisure.* Widely recognized as one of the world's foremost travel photographers, he was the first person to twice receive the Photographer of the Year Award from the Society of American Travel Writers.